Close-up

WORKBOOK

C2

Phillip McElmuray

NATIONAL GEOGRAPHIC
LEARNING

Australia · Brazil · Mexico · Singapore · United Kingdom · United States

NATIONAL GEOGRAPHIC
L E A R N I N G

Close-up C2 Workbook

Phillip McElmuray

Publisher: Gavin McLean

Editorial Manager: Claire Merchant

Commissioning Editor: Kayleigh Buller

Editor: Cathy Rogers

Head of Production: Celia Jones

Content Project Manager: Melissa Beavis

Manufacturing Manager: Eyvett Davis

Text/Cover Designer: MPS Limited

Compositor: Wild Apple Design Ltd

For permission to use material from this text or product, submit all requests online at **cengage.com/permissions**

Further permissions questions can be emailed to **permissionrequest@cengage.com.**

ISBN: 978-1-4080-9838-7

National Geographic Learning
Cheriton House, North Way, Andover, Hampshire,
SP10 5BE United Kingdom

Cengage Learning is a leading provider of customised learning solutions with office locations around the globe, including Singapore, the United Kingdom, Australia, Mexico, Brazil and Japan.

Cengage Learning products are represented in Canada by Nelson Education Ltd.

Visit National Geographic Learning online at **NGL.cengage.com/Closeup**
Visit our corporate website at **cengage.com**

Photo Credits
Cover images: (front cover) Hans Christiansson/Shutterstock Inc, (back cover) MalcolmC/Shutterstock Inc

© Alamy:
6 Westend61 GmbH; **11** Alexey Kotelnikov; **13** Rod Jones; **34** North Wind Picture Archives; **59** Amomentintime; **66** Panda Eye/Cpress Photo Limited; **69** PhotoAlto; **84** Angela Waye; **85** Gregg Vignal; **91** Peter Horree

© Getty Images:
21 Brand X Pictures/Getty Images; **67** Hugh Sitton/Getty Images

© Robert Harding:
27 Werner Bachmeier/Robertharding; **Multiple pages (Learning Focus Icon)** Frank Fox/Okapia

© Shutterstock:
3 Galyna Andrushko; **3** Sylvie Bouchard; **4** John Bill; **4** Dudarev Mikhail; **5** ESB Professional; **7** Syda Productions; **8** Grmarc; **9** Antoniodiaz; **10** Evgeniya Porechenskaya; **10** KPG Payless2; **10** Dotshock; **10** Luminis; **12** Scharfsinn; **14** Mr.Timmi; **15** Pavel L Photo and Video; **18** Ronnie Howard; **19** Jurik Peter; **20** Konrad Mostert; **22** Sfio Cracho; **23** Arthimedes; **24** Michaelpuche; **25** A katz; **26** Rawpixel.com; **28** Wayhome studio; **29** Oneinchpunch; **30** Dirk Ercken; **31** Jacob Lund; **35** Rawpixel.com; **36** Albina Tiplyashina; **38** Maggee; **39** Mihai Simonia; **40** Anastasios71; **41** Robert Kneschke; **42** Alexander Image; **43** ASDF_MEDIA; **44** David Smart; **45** Alexander Vasilyev; **46** Amasterphotographer; **47** Blend Images; **50** Nick Fox; **51** Sergey Nivens; **52** Salajean; **53** Nomad Soul; **54** Marisa Estivill; **55** Altana-studio; **56** ChameleonsEye; **57** Loveischiangrai; **58** Michaeljung; **58** George Rudy; **58** Dean Drobot; **58** Racorn; **58** Andriianov; **60** George Rudy; **61** Bibiphoto; **62** Sielan; **63** Monkey Business Images; **68** Kudla; **68** Maslowski Marcin; **70** Anne Kitzman; **71** Antonio Guillem; **73** G-stockstudio; **74** LiliGraphie; **75** Shane Maritch; **76** Jack Frog; **77** Ilozavr; **78** Kerdkanno; **79** Poznyakov; **82** Eyecan; **83** Icarmen13; **86** Ysbrand Cosijn; **87** MJTH; **88** Fabrik Bilder; **89** Anna Chelnokova; **90** Vchal; **92** Yu Zhang; **94** Jan Cejka; **95** Bodrumsurf; **98** Lydia Vero; **99** LanKS; **Multiple pages (Exam Close-up Icon)** Nikkytok; **Multiple pages (Review Pages)** Pikselstock; **Multiple pages (Review Pages)** Odua Images

Printed in the United Kingdom by CPI Antony Rowe

Print number 07 Print year 2023

Contents

Reading

A Read the *Exam Reminder*. Which questions from the *Exam Task* does it apply to?

_____

B Now complete the *Exam Task*.

Text 1

Can a type of farming affect human behaviour?

The old adage 'You are what you eat' might also apply to what you farm. A study involving Chinese students uncovered striking cognitive differences between those who live in rice-growing provinces and those who reside in areas producing wheat, with the former leaning towards collectivist thinking and the latter being more individualistic. While researchers stop short of concluding that different types of farming regions alone determine behaviour, rather than a range of sociological factors, the study gives us some insight into how an agricultural region shapes a person's character.

The indicators seem to lie in the way crop maintenance shapes human behaviour. For the rice farmers of southern China, successful production relies on interdependence. They are more or less forced to work together to maintain the complex system of planting, irrigating and harvesting rice, so there exists a large network of labour exchanges, in which farmers travel from one plantation to another, helping out where needed. Their cooperation strengthens their sociable traits, which are then passed down to their children. In contrast, wheat production can be carried out almost entirely without the help of another farmer, reducing the need for them to interact with their peers.

The researchers carrying out the study conducted tests on college students in both rice- and wheat-growing regions in order to identify any differences in how they think and view themselves. In one test, subjects were asked to do a word association task. Given the words 'train', 'bus' and 'track', those from rice-growing regions most often paired 'train' and 'track' together, placing focus on the necessity of relationships between things. Those from wheat-growing areas chose 'train' and 'bus', a more analytical choice involving abstract categorisation. Another test involved drawing circles to represent the individual and their network of friends. Students from rice provinces often represented their friends by larger circles than their own, whereas their counterparts drew their representative circles 1.5 millimetres greater on average than the circles for their friends.

Naturally, the researchers investigated other factors that might explain these behavioural differences, such as socioeconomic or cultural differences within China. Only the differences in crop regions, at least in preliminary findings, seemed to account for differences in behaviour. The heads of the study do stress that while the findings are intriguing, the participant pool must be expanded to include actual farmers from those regions.

Exam Reminder

Looking for the main purpose or idea of a text

- The questions about the main purpose of a text will have options that contain ideas mentioned in the text, but which do not necessarily encompass the main idea.
- Look for options that focus on only one particular detail of the text and rule out those options.
- With the last remaining option, make sure the writer discusses this idea throughout the text.

Text 2

'Fearless' woman actually missing a part of her brain

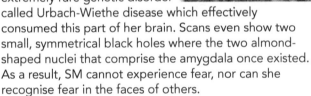

A 44-year-old woman is at the centre of a research study involving the amygdala, a small part of the brain that controls certain emotional responses, specifically fear and anxiety. When 'SM' – an pseudonym to protect her identity – was ten years old, she suffered from an extremely rare genetic disorder called Urbach-Wiethe disease which effectively consumed this part of her brain. Scans even show two small, symmetrical black holes where the two almond-shaped nuclei that comprise the amygdala once existed. As a result, SM cannot experience fear, nor can she recognise fear in the faces of others.

Scientists placed SM in a number of frightening situations in order to monitor her reactions. In one, they guided her through a pet shop replete with snakes and spiders. Oddly, SM had previously professed a fear of snakes to the researchers, so in the pet shop, they were fascinated with her reaction. SM was totally at ease and expressed excitement and curiosity about the snakes, even cradling one in her hands and caressing its scales. When asked to rate her level of fear from one to ten, SM never rated it any higher than two in any of the scenarios she was placed in.

SM was also given an electronic diary so that three times a day she could answer questions related to how she was feeling. During the three months that SM completed the diary, she recorded experiencing a range of emotions, but never the key research element of fear.

The findings of the study could pave the way for new techniques in psychotherapy which focus on reducing the capacity of the amygdala in order to limit the impact of post-traumatic stress disorders. Researchers admit that this treatment would not be without risks, due to the role fear plays in keeping people safe. SM has been the victim of numerous crimes as an adult, remaining calm throughout all incidents, but she might have avoided potentially dangerous situations in the first place had she possessed the ability to feel fear.

Read the two passages from a scientific magazine, then answer questions according to the information given in each passage.

Text 1

1 What is the main purpose of the passage?
  a to explain how food affects people
  b to profile types of individuals
  c to compare farming techniques
  d to contrast two differing lifestyles

2 Which factor accounts for rice farmers' interdependence?
  a regional challenges
  b competition from wheat farmers
  c labour requirements
  d their inherent nature

3 In paragraph 3, the **counterparts** are
  a wheat farmers.
  b friends of study participants.
  c other study participants.
  d the circle drawings.

4 Which statement is correct regarding the researchers' beliefs about the study?
  a They are not quite satisfied with the results.
  b They feel certain of farming's effects on behaviour.
  c They believe the findings cannot be correct.
  d They wish they'd studied a range of factors.

Text 2

5 What is the passage mainly about?
  a finding the causes of Urbach-Wiethe disease
  b studying neurological processes provoked by fear
  c limiting the effects of fearful situations
  d the role of the amygdala in the brain

6 Researchers felt that SM's interaction with the pet shop snakes was
  a intriguingly intimate.
  b unsurprising given her condition.
  c extremely dangerous and worrying.
  d surprisingly dispassionate.

7 What was the diary used for?
  a as a way for SM to record her emotions
  b as a system for ranking the things SM felt
  c as a list of SM's daily activities
  d as a tool to help SM feel fear

8 What can be inferred about how the scientists will further their research?
  a They intend to discover a way to switch off the amygdala.
  b They do not want to eliminate the ability to feel fear altogether.
  c They do not wish to alter the abilities of the amygdala.
  d They will seek a cure for what initially disabled SM.

Vocabulary

A Complete the sentences with these words and the prefixes *ab-*, *dys-*, *mal-* or *mis-*.

adjusted   behave   errant   function   functional

1 Despite coming from a slightly _____ family, Robert was a well-mannered gentleman.
2 Debra's parents scolded her harshly for her _____ behaviour during her sister's wedding.
3 Often prisoners are _____ on release and a period of acclimatisation is required.
4 The machine had a _____ and it didn't finish printing the pages.
5 The teacher told the children not to _____ while she stepped out of class for a moment.

B Match the behaviour described by the speakers to an adjective from the list.

1 'He told me they had found a cure for baldness and I actually believed him!' ☐
2 'It's hard to get a reaction out of Roger; nothing seems to interest him.' ☐
3 'When my dad gets an idea in his head, no one can make him change his mind.' ☐
4 'The flight attendant was friendly and patient, and she really made the flight a joy.' ☐
5 'I hate working with Thomas because he does things without asking anyone first.' ☐
6 'I couldn't believe how rude that man was. He should have been kicked out.' ☐
7 'Sarah is very careful with how she arranges her desk and how she plans her schedule.' ☐
8 'I've got a bad feeling about this area. I think we should go back.' ☐

a obstinate
b amiable
c uneasy
d apathetic
e meticulous
f obnoxious
g compulsive
h gullible

C Circle the correct words.

Patience truly is a virtue

A study in the late 1960s demonstrated how children can become more (**1**) principled / neurotic and self-disciplined if they resist temptation regularly. A single marshmallow was placed in front of a child to monitor how they would (**2**) exert / conduct themselves in tempting situations. They were told they could eat that marshmallow immediately or have two if they waited 15 minutes. Most children said they would wait, but they couldn't resist and polished off the sweet quickly. The only way some children could keep a cool (**3**) face / head and avoid eating the marshmallow was to look away or cover their eyes. Researchers kept track of the children as they aged, and the ones who couldn't wait were more (**4**) compatible / vulnerable to problems such as obesity and were also more
(**5**) tempted / prone to suffering from drug addiction and severe behavioural (**6**) disorders / dysfunctions in adulthood.

D Complete the sentences by writing one noun or preposition in each gap.

1 Don't flirt with Matt. You shouldn't lead him _____ when you know you don't want to date him.

2 This machine has broken down six times this week – it's a real _____ in the neck.

3 Larry and I have known each other for years and we're on quite good _____.

4 I can't imagine Professor Burns cancelling the test today; that's very _____ of character for him.

5 After spending years being single and living in the city, Maria finally settled _____, got married and moved to the suburbs.

6 We've been friends all our lives; we shouldn't let a stupid argument come _____ us.

7 If you're too hard _____ your employees, you'll breed resentment.

8 His behaviour at dinner was atrocious; it was simply _____ belief.

E Read the *Exam Reminder* and complete the *Exam Task*.

Exam Task

Choose the word or phrase that best completes the sentence.

1 Bill finally told his professor about the cheating, as he had to get it off his _____.

  a shoulders   b head

  c chest   d mouth

2 To assume the new government will just make our country's problems worse is quite _____ of you.

  a poised   b meticulous

  c scrupulous   d cynical

3 The _____ result gave George great cause for alarm.

  a maladjusted   b dysfunctional

  c aberrant   d abnormal

4 Jill would never make such a thoughtless decision. She's far too _____.

  a obnoxious   b cynical

  c eloquent   d scrupulous

5 As Lisa was touched by Martin's generosity, she felt she should make a _____ gesture.

  a philosophical   b reciprocal

  c gullible   d vulnerable

Exam Reminder

Eliminating wrong answers

• Review all the choices for a particular gap and cross out the ones you know are wrong.

• Narrow your choices further by trying each remaining option in the gap until there's only one left.

• Be sure to reread the sentence with your chosen word to ensure that it makes sense.

6 It wasn't my colleague's fault that the study failed, so I decided to _____ up for him.

  a stay   b get

  c stick   d work

7 Although Gail thought she should have won first place, she _____ her pride and congratulated her rival.

  a exerted   b swallowed

  c bore   d aroused

8 You don't have to take part in the tournament. I would never make you do something _____ your will.

  a beyond   b towards

  c over   d against

Grammar

Review of Present & Present Perfect Tenses

A Complete the sentences with the correct form of these words.

> always peer   conduct   drift   just settle   treat   vent

1 Monica and I last spoke a year ago and now I really feel like we _____ apart.
2 Don't go into that conference room; the boss _____ his anger for the last half an hour.
3 The famous psychiatrist Dr Carl _____ many people with severe mental illnesses over the years.
4 I don't like the new research assistant because he _____ over my shoulder.
5 Angela and Mark _____ their research study for nearly three years now.
6 I've been searching for a research topic all day and I think I _____ on one.

B Write sentences using present tenses according to the prompts.

An action that happened at an unspecified time in the past

1 they / test / range of hypotheses

_____

2 Rashid / complete / the trial study

_____

A situation happening now

3 the scientist / analyse / the data

_____

4 I / put / the samples / into the machine

_____

An action with duration emphasised

5 Leon / interview / subjects / hours

_____

6 Ms Clarkson / working / all morning

_____

A scientific fact

7 the brain / process / images / 13 milliseconds

_____

A stative verb

8 he / appreciate / your hard work

_____

Simple & Continuous tenses

C Complete the sentences with the correct form of the verbs in brackets.

1 The food _____ (**taste**) terrible and Sonia didn't eat another bite.
2 They _____ (**drive**) in circles for half an hour by the time John pulled out a map.
3 While Henry _____ (**taste**) the sauce, Paul was checking on the turkey in the oven.
4 I know Helen's family; we _____ (**meet**) before.
5 Kyle _____ (**drive**) all the way to Sarah's house when he realised he had forgotten the gift.
6 Hurry up! We _____ (**meet**) the Jensons in 45 minutes.
7 _____ (**you / see**) Michael becoming a nuclear physicist?
8 We _____ (**not walk**) for four hours; we left at nine and it's 11.30 now.

Used to, Would & Will; Auxiliaries

D Each sentence has an incorrect word or phrase. Cross it out and write the correct word or phrase. More than one answer may be possible.

1 She would be a research assistant, but now she supervises the lab.   _____
2 That's strange; Barb used never to talk to her neighbours across the street.   _____
3 They ran the results through the computer and, after they have, they wrote a detailed report.   _____
4 Henry didn't used to be so difficult to work with, but he's been under a lot of pressure.   _____
5 In the mornings, my dog would always beg me to take him for a walk. He loves going out.   _____
6 He rarely made a mistake in his research, but when he does, he wouldn't admit it so readily.   _____
7 Marcos was being a teacher at that school, but he retired a few years back.   _____
8 We're soaking up the rays on the beach, just like we did every time we go on holiday.   _____

E Read the *Exam Reminder* and complete the *Exam Task*.

Exam Task

Read the article about false memory research. For questions **1 – 8**, read the text below and think of the word which best fits each space. Use only **one** word in each space.

How strong language changes memories

Researchers (**1**) _____ been studying the psychological phenomenon known as false memory since the mid-1970s. The first experiments involved having participants watch videos of car accidents and, after they (**2**) _____, researchers would ask some of them the question, 'How fast were the cars going when they smashed into each other?' Other participants were asked the same question, but the verb *smashed* was changed to either *hit*, *collided*, *bumped* or *contacted*, and depending on the verb, participants (**3**) _____ answer differently. In another experiment, researchers asked participants to recall certain details about the accidents. Even though broken glass had (**4**) _____ appeared in any video, some would purport that they had in fact seen glass break if the researcher used a more dynamic verb in the question.

Nowadays, researchers (**5**) _____ studying the phenomenon to help people recall events in their lives so painful that they had (**6**) _____ burying their memories of them for decades. This phenomenon also raises questions about the accuracy of witness testimonials in the legal arena. In the past, courts (**7**) _____ to often accept eyewitness testimonies as unassailable fact, yet research (**8**) _____ since shown that our memories can be manipulated by a multitude of factors, such as a barrister's choice of words or aggressive witness cross-examination during the trial.

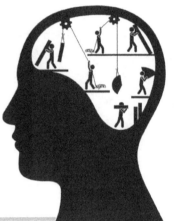

Listening

A Read the *Exam Reminder*. What key words would you underline in the *Exam Task* questions?

_____

B 1.1 ▶️ Listen and complete the Exam Task.

Exam Task

You will hear three different extracts. For questions **1 – 6**, choose the answer (**a**, **b** or **c**) which fits best according to what you hear. There are two questions for each extract. You will hear the extracts twice.

Extract 1
You will hear a woman discussing workplace bullying.

1 What reason does the woman give for bullies to bully?
  a They're bad at their jobs.
  b They've simply been around the office too long.
  c They're looking to improve their standing with supervisors.

2 The woman believes companies should face up to bullying because
  a the majority of companies now have anti-bullying procedures.
  b companies who put a stop to bullying operate more efficiently.
  c bullying victims are beginning to display serious health problems.

Extract 2
You will hear a sociologist being interviewed about why people give.

3 The sociologist says people are less likely to donate to charity when
  a the donation is for a single person.
  b the charity focuses on statistics.
  c the charity declares how well it does.

4 How does the sociologist feel charities should change approach?
  a They should make it a more personal experience.
  b They should employ celebrities to contact donors.
  c They should include more causes in their charitable efforts.

Extract 3
You will hear a man describing how jealousy plays a role in self-esteem.

5 The man notes that previous studies on self-esteem often
  a focused on a person's genes.
  b focused on aggression.
  c ignored the presence of substance abuse.

6 What does the man find most upsetting about how jealousy affects friendship?
  a the impact that it has on a particular gender
  b the fact that jealous people overly protect their friends
  c how it degrades a friendship beyond the point of benefit

C 1.2 ▶️ Listen again and check your answers.

Writing: an essay (1)

A Complete the table with these words.

apathetic   constructive   content   discontented   dissatisfied
meticulous   neurotic   open   positive   sympathetic
violent   withdrawn

Well-adjusted individuals are often ...	Maladjusted individuals can be ...

Learning Reminder

Planning & organising a discursive essay

- Plan your essay before you start, as that will help you focus and organise your thoughts.
- Read the topic carefully and make sure you understand it. Jot down some notes with appropriate ideas and vocabulary.
- Begin your discursive essay by restating the topic. Write clear topic sentences to introduce your subsequent paragraphs.
- Use a formal, impersonal style and connect your ideas with suitable linking words.

B Read the students' notes for the corresponding topics. Did they address the topics appropriately? What changes would you make to them?

1 They say a positive mind leads to a positive body. How might that way of thinking improve our physical self? What tends to happen when the opposite is true as regards the mind?

having a good outlook on life, desire to do good for oneself, desire to eat better and exercise

2 Research concludes that our formative years are our best chance for positive development. What happens to those who missed out on that due to dysfunction in the family? What help is there for them?

imperative that children have positive home lives, investing time in their development ensures a happy life

3 Punishing students who misbehave seems par for the course. But what happens when the punishment does nothing to correct behaviour? What forms of punishment might be more constructive for students?

of course no one likes punishment, punishment is not meant to be enjoyable

C Write topic sentences for these two paragraphs. What questions do you think were in the topic of the essay that these paragraphs belong in?

1
_____
_____

A case in point is when young people are completely absorbed in social media. They communicate with friends only online, have little contact with the world around them and know very little about the challenges that face less advantaged individuals.

2
_____
_____

For instance, doing voluntary work can help acquaint young people with people who struggle in their daily lives. In some cases, youths can forge a bond with a member of the community and learn new, fascinating and perhaps painful things about society that may in turn help to improve it.

D Read and complete the *Exam Task*. Don't forget to use the *Useful Expressions* on page 17 of your Student's Book.

▶ Writing Reference p. 205 in Student's Book

Exam Task

American actor and social activist Edward James Olmos once said, 'Education is the vaccine for violence.' If this is true, why might a student resort to violence in an educational facility? What are some ways to reduce violence in schools? Support your opinion with reasons and examples.

Write your **essay** in 280–320 words.

Reading

A Read the *Exam Reminder*. What key words would you underline in the *Exam Task* questions?

B Now complete the *Exam Task*.

Are robots taking over?

A Elliot

It never ceases to amaze me how we hurl ourselves toward a human-free society at lightning speed. Despite endless articles and even award-winning films about how we're losing touch with ourselves and our humanity, out roll driverless cars and automated trains. I might not be able to speak for all of society, but I think I've got quite a good grasp on the human psyche and, for whatever reason, we are not terribly fond of robots. I recently read a survey about people's feelings on artificial intelligence and I believe it perfectly encapsulates the current mood. Around 70 per cent of people are happy to allow robots to do ordinary, boring jobs such as crop monitoring. But when those activities encroach upon our private space, for instance having a robot maid, only around half of respondents were in agreement with it. Give a robot a scalpel and have it perform surgery, and only a quarter of people would hop on the table. I'm only shocked that it's not zero per cent – whoever is part of that 25 per cent must be completely mad, as far as I'm concerned.

B Josephine

Is our trepidation about artificial intelligence every bit as manufactured as the technology itself? Our cinematic experiences may very well be culpable for embedding most of this fear of the unknown into our minds. However, if you toss that aside and peruse current articles about real-life AI, you still might find yourself trembling slightly. News of driverless public transport popping up in major European cities does little to assuage our anxiety because, let's face it, you can't help but imagine what could happen if things went awry. A simple malfunction could place two commuter-packed buses in a head-on collision or cause a brake failure in a speeding underground train which cannot be stopped by human intervention. Honestly, just like our food labels should tell us if what we're eating is genetically modified, so should a bus or train have signage saying it is operated only by machine. Then we can decide if we want to step foot inside or wait for a conventional public transport vehicle to pull up.

C Ronald

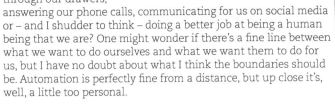

I would postulate that we have a bitter-sweet love affair with automation. Do we want robots to wash our dishes, clean up our mess, vacuum and polish our flooring, do our laundry, and even fold, iron and hang up our finely tailored clothing? I would give an affirmative response to that. And who wouldn't, really? But do we want them buzzing around our homes, rummaging through our drawers, answering our phone calls, communicating for us on social media or – and I shudder to think – doing a better job at being a human being that we are? One might wonder if there's a fine line between what we want to do ourselves and what we want them to do for us, but I have no doubt about what I think the boundaries should be. Automation is perfectly fine from a distance, but up close it's, well, a little too personal.

D Laura

We've been fascinated with robots and artificial intelligence for decades now. I remember watching Stanley Kubrick's 2001: A Space Odyssey when I was a child, terrified at how the ship's sentient robot, HAL 9000, usurped control of the vessel from the film's protagonist, Dr David Bowman. Society at large has a latent fear that robots will do that in real life, but I would advise them to remember that in this important masterpiece of Kubrick's, Bowman prevailed in the end. Of course, our fears of out-of-control computers subjugating humans make nice fodder for the science-fiction genre, but let's not lose our heads. I'm confident that mankind will only ever devise an artificially intelligent device just powerful enough to serve us, but never powerful enough to supplant us.

You are going to read four people's opinions about artificial intelligence. For questions **1 – 10**, choose from the people (**A – D**). The people may be chosen more than once.

Which person gives each of these opinions about artificial intelligence?

1 We should be clear on what robots are and aren't allowed to do.
2 An analysis of fiction concerning tales of man against machine would ease our fears of robots.
3 The more intimate the chore, the more unnerved we become about robots doing it.
4 Our fears of robots may have been overblown by fictional stories.
5 Simple awareness is important in order for people to make informed choices.
6 Mankind is too aware of the threat machines pose to allow them to be problematic.
7 It's impossible to avoid thinking of the worst-case scenario regarding robot-controlled tasks.
8 It's a common desire to want menial tasks done via automation.
9 That anyone would leave their well-being in the hands of robots is particularly appalling.
10 Our fears of machines are always there, if not always easily visible.

Vocabulary

A Complete each pair of sentences with these words.

censors sensors

1 The film was far too racy for prime-time television and the _____ wouldn't allow it to be broadcast until after midnight.
2 Many paper towel dispensers are equipped with _____ that allow you to get paper towels automatically.

ingenious ingenuous

3 The _____ child reached out to shake the robot's hand without any fear of having her hand crushed.
4 Whoever came up with this _____ idea to manufacture handbags from disused plastic is a true environmentalist.

decompose disintegrate

5 If no one removes that dead whale from the beach, its body will soon _____ and produce a nasty stench.
6 Placing a polystyrene cup into nail polish remover will cause it to _____ in a matter of seconds.

emit omit

7 The researcher had to prove that he did not purposefully _____ pertinent data from the report.
8 Stars of average size, like our sun, _____ more energy in one second than mankind has consumed in its entire existence.

B Complete the words in the sentences.

1 The p_ _ _ _ _ _ _ of the school announced that there would be no class today due to severe weather.
2 Although you can take steps to reduce the impact of malaria infections across the globe, it will be very difficult to e_ _ _ _ _ _ _ _ it entirely.
3 Although functional, durable and perhaps fashionable in a different era, the grey, utterly u_ _ _ _ _ _ _ _ _ _ clothing made its wearers look robotic and emotionless.
4 Hearsay and conjecture aren't going to prove your case in court; what you need is some t_ _ _ _ _ _ proof that the perpetrator is guilty.
5 The sun generates heat by forcing hydrogen atoms to bond with one another and release energy through a process of physics called nuclear f_ _ _ _ _.
6 Marie added a spoonful of salt to her pasta sauce and stirred it until it completely d_ _ _ _ _ _ _.
7 I'm afraid your ideas are a bit too r_ _ _ _ _ _ _ _ _ _ for my taste; I prefer more conventional solutions.
8 Because Darren forgot to d_ _ _ _ _ important numbers from the equation, his results were grossly overstated.

C Complete the sentences with phrases formed from one of these words and two extra words for every gap.

forth	front	go	little	more	safe	time	wear

1 There's so much _____ on these sleeves that I'll probably have to buy a new jacket soon.

2 He's out of surgery, but it's going to be a bit _____ for the next few hours.

3 My new smartphone has quite a sleek design, but the interface is _____ the same as my old one.

4 They argued _____ until they got tired and stopped talking altogether.

5 I just got in touch with Paula and, after her harrowing ordeal while traversing the Alps, I'm happy to say she returned _____.

6 It was taking John hours to put his disassembled laptop back together, but _____, he eventually finished.

7 The grand opening of the residential tower would have been heralded as a success, except that many window features had been put on _____.

8 The scientist is chaotic and unorthodox in his methods, but _____, he never fails to impress.

D Circle the correct words.

1 The compound is on complete lockdown due to a serious security code / breach.

2 The results of most search vehicles / engines are ordered by the number of times they've been viewed.

3 If tensions between the two countries rise any further, I fear they will be on / at the brink of war.

4 Do you think artificial technology / intelligence will ever be smarter than the human mind?

5 After the coach fired the starting pistol, the sprinters were off / up and running.

6 A computer's operating engine / system manages and organises software programs and hardware devices.

7 3D printing is still in its beginning / infancy; imagine what it will be like in 15 years.

8 If you're still using dial-up to access the internet, I'm afraid you're quite beyond / behind the times!

E Read the *Exam Reminder* and complete the *Exam Task*.

Exam Reminder

Identifying collocations
- Look at the gaps, and check what part of speech is required and if it is part of a collocation, idiom or set expression.
- Read the sentence with your chosen answer to make sure you have made the correct choice.

Exam Task

For questions **1 – 8**, read the text below and decide which answer (**a, b, c** or **d**) best fits each gap.

Learning more than how to surf

Technology's continual surge forward is well evidenced in television, advertising and multimedia, so it's not difficult to (**1**) _____ that the general public's knowledge of computers must develop at the same pace. The level of computer (**2**) _____ required to succeed in life is hardly limited to emailing, surfing the web and having a basic knowledge of Microsoft Word. A seasoned employee is likely to be well versed in the ins and (**3**) _____ of computer software and hardware, as least to some extent. In fact, former UK culture minister Ed Vaizey recently postulated that knowing how a computer works would be '(**4**) _____ a par with a knowledge of the arts and humanities'. He also suggested that knowing a bit about computer coding would acquaint people with the digital world in a way that would allow them to become an active participant in its (**5**) _____ process.

Acquiring above-average skills in computer usage isn't even all that's required, because as computer systems and programs become (**6**) _____, users have to learn new sets of keystrokes, menu options and interfacing. It goes far beyond basic office management and data processing; medical equipment is often tethered to a computer system which aids doctors and nurses in (**7**) _____ vital data. While there may still be some fields of employment in which computers take a back (**8**) _____ to the work (think fishing), there isn't a job, field or profession that wouldn't benefit from a digital revolution. Come to think of it, even the smallest of fishing boats are likely to be fitted with GPS devices!

1	a	reduce	b	deduce	c	induce	d produce
2	a	fluency	b	familiarity	c	literacy	d mastery
3	a	forwards	b	downs	c	ups	d outs
4	a	on	b	with	c	to	d in
5	a	customary	b	evolutionary	c	revolutionary	d contemporary
6	a	archaic	b	conventional	c	obsolete	d unfashionable
7	a	interpreting	b	translating	c	illuminating	d decoding
8	a	stage	b	seat	c	row	d door

Grammar

Future Forms

A Write sentences using future forms according to the prompts.

1 you / need / a ride / the airport (**formal question**)

_____

2 I / not surf / net / until / I / finish / assignment (**determination**)

_____

3 they / not share / data / unauthorised personnel (**obligation**)

_____

4 the director / promote / Julie / lead scientist (**formal announcement**)

_____

5 by the time / John / arrive / guests / leave (**completed action before a certain time**)

_____

B Complete the sentences with the correct future form of the verbs in brackets.

1 After the medicine has taken effect, you _____ (**fall**) asleep in a matter of seconds.

2 While you're testing the samples, I _____ (**enter**) the readings into the database.

3 By the time this century is over, we _____ (**explore**) our entire solar system.

4 Until you've completely finished your meal, you _____ (**remain**) firmly seated at this table.

5 When the indicator has moved all the way to the right, the process _____ (**completely finish**).

Verbs with a future implication; Adjectives and phrases expressing the future; Future in the past

C Circle the correct words.

1 I hope to hear / hearing from you in a few short months.

2 Everyone is excited because they're just about to / about to just make an important announcement.

3 The team dread the mission to / that the mission will be a total failure.

4 I don't foresee there to be / being any delays in the delivery.

5 I'm afraid a move to make mass redundancies brews / is brewing in the company.

6 The entrepreneurs plan utilising / to utilise the expertise of Nobel prize-winning scientists.

7 We don't envisage / fear any potential life-threatening issues arising.

8 You must find a solution soon; everyone is counting / expecting on you.

9 We are sure to / sure find a satisfactory solution to the problem if we all work together.

10 Pat dreaded to go / going back to see the doctor because he was worried about the test results.

D Rewrite the sentences using future in the past forms.

1 The ideas he's generating will revolutionise farming technology.

_____

2 Sorry, but he's never going to find a cure for baldness!

_____

3 The actions world leaders take now will affect generations of people.

_____

4 Something is going to happen that will revolutionise our working lives.

_____

E Read the *Exam Reminder* and complete the *Exam Task*.

Exam Task

Read the passage, then select the word or phrase that fills the blank in both meaning and grammar.

The future place in space

Many people wonder if what they saw in *Total Recall*, a film in which humans inhabited Mars, (**1**) _____ happen one day in their lifetime. While space exploration mostly centres around travel to Mars, scientists have set their sights on destinations further out in our solar system once the technology to do so gets (**2**) _____ to speed. In fact, when mankind (**3**) _____ the fourth planet from the sun, we will have likely found ways to reach arguably far more intriguing celestial bodies, at least in terms of their potential to sustain life.

One such destination is Europa, one of Jupiter's four Galilean moons. Current technology has revealed that its ice-covered surface contains vast amounts of liquid water underneath, and space explorers (**4**) _____ finding extra-terrestrial life there. Both NASA and ESA recently announced that they are (**5**) _____ probes to Europa. Unfortunately, radiation levels around Europa would wreak havoc with the probes' instruments, preventing an actual landing. Instead, the probes will conduct fly-by missions while orbiting Jupiter, and they are (**6**) _____ to make some tantalising discoveries.

1	**a** will	**b** can	**c** would	**d** did
2	**a** on	**b** up	**c** over	**d** round
3	**a** reaches	**b** has reached	**c** will reach	**d** will be reaching
4	**a** are anticipating	**b** anticipate	**c** will anticipate	**d** have anticipated
5	**a** to send	**b** send	**c** will send	**d** sent
6	**a** almost	**b** about	**c** bound	**d** indeed

Listening

A Read the *Exam Reminder*. Which task from the *Exam Task* requires you to listen for facts, and which requires you to listen for opinions?

_____

B 🔊 2.1 Listen and complete the *Exam Task*.

Exam Task

You will hear five short extracts in which different people talk about their experiences with computers.

Task 1

For questions **1 – 5**, choose from the list (**A – H**) what belief each speaker holds about computers.

Task 2

For questions **6 – 10**, choose from the list (**A – H**) what experience each speaker has had with computers.

You will hear the recording twice. While you listen, you must complete both tasks.

A frugal purchasing	**1** Speaker 1	☐
B better builds	**2** Speaker 2	☐
C unnecessary devices	**3** Speaker 3	☐
D system preservation	**4** Speaker 4	☐
E sceptical of tech professionals	**5** Speaker 5	☐
F passing fad		
G efficient workhorse		
H informed decision-making		

A dizzying amount of choice	**6** Speaker 1	☐
B addictive nature	**7** Speaker 2	☐
C sluggish performance	**8** Speaker 3	☐
D stationary usage	**9** Speaker 4	☐
E physical discomfort	**10** Speaker 5	☐
F frustrating beginnings		
G debilitating anxiety		
H hands-on servicing		

C 🔊 2.2 Listen again and check your answers.

Writing: a review (1)

A Decide if the statements are fact (F), opinion (O) or both fact and opinion (B).

1 I recently attended a thoroughly entertaining expo in London which featured all the latest technological gadgets. ☐

2 For anyone who's interested in attending, it runs until the end of this week. ☐

3 The event covered what seemed like half a football field, roughly speaking. ☐

4 It's mesmerising to experience the virtual worlds that exist in these games. ☐

5 Some things had me scratching my head about how useful they might be for the market. ☐

6 The tech expo was relatively inexpensive to attend, as I only paid 12 euros for entry. ☐

7 There were many tech devices on display, such as watches, glasses, bracelets, belts and even gloves. ☐

8 The site was expansive; it was set in a refurbished warehouse in an industrial district in London. ☐

Learning Reminder

Understanding the content of a review

• Remember that reviews present facts and opinions together in an engaging and informal format.

• The facts should consist of answers to *wh-* questions as well as specific details of what you experienced.

• Remember to organise your review clearly. Include an introduction informing readers of what the review is about, a main body containing discussion of specific aspects and a conclusion containing the writer's overall opinion and a recommendation.

B Use these adjectives to complete the opinion statements.

> attentive   avid   dazzling   impractical   informative   obsessed   preoccupied   welcoming

1 The tech company's representatives were _____, _____ and _____, but one of them seemed a bit _____ with something else.

2 The multimedia presentations were _____ to look at, but I found what they demonstrated to be _____.

3 My brother is a(n) _____ gamer, but my sister thinks he's _____!

C Read the partial review. Use these words and phrases to rewrite the phrases in bold.

> exorbitant   newbie   proficient   promotional   steep learning curve   tech expo   tech wiz   wearable

When it comes to using technology, I have to admit I'm **not someone who's used a lot of it before** _____. But I wanted to attend **one of those places where they feature the latest in technology** _____, so I decided to go with a friend. While perusing the floor, I came across a booth with a number of **devices that you can wear on your head or body** _____. I tried one on, but honestly, I had a bit of trouble using it. A representative who was **very good and highly skilled** _____ in its use helped me get started. I thought for sure it would **take hours and hours just to learn basic tasks** _____. However, after about 20 minutes, I had mastered it and I really felt like **someone who knows everything about technology** _____! The representatives handed me some **information that lists the device's selling points** _____, but I was hesitant to invest in one. It had **a price tag that was far too high for me to ever be able to afford** _____, so I'll stick with my cheap smartphone.

D Read and complete the *Exam Task*. Don't forget to use the *Useful Expressions* on page 31 of your Student's book.

↻ **Writing Reference p. 206 in Student's Book** ▶

Exam Task

You are the writer of a blog about technology, and you write about new devices, advances in the field and events that you attend. You recently attended a tech expo in London, and you would like to write a review of the expo and post it on your blog. Describe your experience at the expo, and say what you enjoyed the most and why you felt it was worth visiting.

Write your **review** in 280–320 words.

Review 1   Units 1 & 2

Vocabulary

A   Choose the correct answers.

1 She's been a member of the site for years, but she's no longer an active _____.

  a customer   **b** handler

  c operator   **d** user

2 Films add an element of fright to their storylines by showing robots with scarily powerful _____ intelligence.

  a fake   **b** plastic

  c artificial   **d** synthetic

3 If you want to make it in the field of technology, study hard and stay ahead of the _____.

  a twist   **b** circle

  c spin   **d** curve

4 Following the collapse of the Berlin Wall in 1989, it took less than a year for Germany to be _____.

  a unified   **b** combined

  c joined   **d** merged

5 The tendency is to respond to anger with anger, but in these situations, it pays to keep a cool _____.

  a brain   **b** mind

  c head   **d** top

6 Most people are _____ to believe that girls and boys like certain toys when they are young.

  a hardened   **b** acclimated

  c conditioned   **d** accustomed

7 Don't _____ him on to join a gang: nothing could be worse for him!

  a egg   **b** toast

  c butter   **d** knife

8 Until emergency crews stablised the reactor, the country was on the _____ of disaster.

  a side   **b** precipice

  c edge   **d** brink

9 I'm not surprised that your brother is angry; you spent half an hour _____ him up about an issue he cares about deeply.

  a spinning   **b** turning

  c winding   **d** twirling

10 You're still using a Windows 7 operating system? You're so _____ the times!

  a out   **b** behind

  c off   **d** under

11 If you were to appoint Jean to the head of the committee, she would be on _____ nine.

  a cloud   **b** sky

  c heaven   **d** fog

12 The magazine's issues have been placed in an electronic archive, so you'll have decades of material _____ your fingertips.

  a at   **b** under

  c within   **d** round

13 Scientists think travelling to Mars will be within _____ in 25 years.

  a handle   **b** reach

  c grasp   **d** hold

14 Your remote control isn't working because it isn't connecting with the _____ on the TV properly.

  a beam   **b** sensor

  c radar   **d** antenna

15 The neighbours were once close friends, but after one moved, they _____ apart.

  a floated   **b** drifted

  c strayed   **d** wandered

16 The secret was causing Amy much stress and she had to get it off her _____.

  a chest   **b** body

  c face   **d** shoulders

17 Lisa was upset with her friend for talking about her behind her _____.

  a back   **b** side

  c head   **d** neck

18 With his boss being so temperamental, it took Joseph a while to _____ up the courage to ask for a pay rise.

  a run   **b** drive

  c pluck   **d** act

19 Helen thought her dog had run away forever, so naturally she was elated to see him back home safe and _____.

  a sound   **b** sight

  c hearing   **d** noise

20 It's just a minor computer glitch; the system will be _____ and running in five minutes.

  a on   **b** off

  c up   **d** over

Grammar

B Choose the correct answers.

1 We'll let you know the details _____ they're made available to us.

   a just as   **b** so long

   c until   **d** as soon as

2 They're better behaved now, but before they _____, we found them quite a handful.

   a are   **b** were

   c did   **d** had

3 Dad made it abundantly clear – you are _____ him as soon as you arrive.

   a to calling   **b** to call

   c call   **d** calling

4 I'm going to put a request in for you, but before I _____, I need your signature on the form.

   a am   **b** do

   c will   **d** would

5 You had better hurry to the stadium – all the best seats _____ taken by now.

   a are being   **b** will have been

   c have been   **d** are

6 I'm sure I can win the election this year, but I _____ on your support.

   a am bound   **b** foresee

   c am counting   **d** anticipate

7 She _____ as if she had the complete confidence of her staff.

   a hadn't been feeling **b** hadn't felt

   c didn't feel   **d** wasn't feeling

8 The negative atmosphere in the office meant a round of dismissals was probably _____.

   a about   **b** upcoming

   c bound   **d** looming

9 Scientists everywhere _____ the alarm over climate change for decades now.

   a sound   **b** are sounding

   c have been sounding **d** have sounded

10 Kyle and George _____ be close colleagues until George's transfer.

   a will   **b** used to

   c would   **d** used

11 Be careful with how you use this lever; it _____ the steering.

   a will control   **b** controls

   c is controlling   **d** controlled

12 They could tell what their teacher _____ by the sour look on her face.

   a is thinking   **b** thinks

   c thought   **d** was thinking

13 Don't turn the computer off … I _____ to check some data.

   a just about   **b** just

   c was just about   **d** about

14 He yelled at his noisy neighbours to turn down their music and, after he _____, it got a bit quieter.

   a was   **b** is

   c did   **d** done

15 By the time Roger arrived, they _____ the agenda for hours.

   a discussed   **b** had discussed

   c had been discussing **d** were discussing

16 Sometimes we _____ behaviour in animals that's quite similar to our own.

   a are seeing   **b** see

   c have seen   **d** were seeing

17 Before they fell out with each other, they _____ each other their most personal secrets.

   a would tell   **b** tell

   c will tell   **d** would be telling

18 He brewed a huge pot of coffee as soon as he got up, as he _____ every day of the week.

   a will   **b** does

   c has   **d** is

19 The panel _____ your proposal at the moment and will contact you in the coming weeks.

   a is considering   **b** considers

   c has considered   **d** will be considering

20 Sarah can't leave the office _____ she finishes the report for the boss.

   a as soon as   **b** just about to

   c while   **d** until

Use of English

C Read the text below and decide which answer (a, b, c or d) best fits each gap.

Chimpanzees and you

Some may be elated to hear this and others a tad (1) _____, but the DNA of chimpanzees and humans differs by only around one per cent, making them more similar to us than (2) _____ gorillas. While they don't (3) _____ themselves entirely like humans, they exhibit behaviours and emotions originally thought only to be expressed by humans. They have a strong sense of community and are rather (4) _____ when a human they know enters the room, as can be (5) ____ from their jumping up and down. Their facial musculature resembles ours very closely, as is witnessed when they smile, express worry or (6) _____ their anger. While we and chimpanzees may be (7) _____ the same wavelength in some respects, there are huge differences. Even the most talented chimpanzee is no match for human intelligence and there isn't even a (8) _____ possibility that they will speak – they lack the vocal tracts necessary for language.

1	a	impassive	b	uneasy	c	overjoyed	d	inflexible
2	a	even	b	fewer	c	less	d	more
3	a	exert	b	assert	c	arouse	d	conduct
4	a	compulsive	b	adamant	c	cynical	d	jubilant
5	a	deducted	b	eroded	c	eradicated	d	deduced
6	a	vent	b	escape	c	conjure	d	brew
7	a	on	b	at	c	with	d	inside
8	a	vast	b	far	c	distant	d	remote

D Complete the text with the correct form of the words in bold.

The 'Silent Twins'

June and Jennifer Gibbons were twin sisters known as 'the Silent Twins' due to their slightly (1) _____ habit of speaking only to each other and to not anyone else. Born in Barbados, their family relocated to Haverfordwest in Wales when they were infants, and their ethnic differences made (2) _____ with the local community quite difficult. The two girls were (3) _____ during their youth, a result of their being ostracised from their community yet needing companionship. Making matters worse was the (4) _____ language that the sisters used to speak to each other; it was a mixture of English and their native language.

Although bullied at school, the two hardly had (5) _____ youths; they enjoyed writing fiction and dreamt of being writers. Their first novels, however, failed to attract much literary attention and, in a sad twist of events, they turned to a life of crime and exhibited even more (6) _____ behaviour. The twin sisters eventually ended up in a mental health facility, and after much fruitless analysis and observation, staff concluded that their condition was seemingly (7) _____. It wasn't until one sister, Jennifer, passed away that June was able to live a normal life. What was certainly true about the sisters is that throughout their troubled lives together, they loved and trusted each other (8) _____.

NORMAL

INTEGRATE

SEPARATE

INTELLIGENT

SPENT

ERRANT

CURE

CONDITION

E Read the text below and think of the word which best fits each gap. Use only one word in each gap.

Exoplanet weather

In 1992, radio astronomers Aleksander Wolszczan and Dale Frail (**1**) _____ listening intently to the night sky. As part of their jobs, they (**2**) _____ to do this night after night in search of anomalous sounds. One night, they made a thrilling discovery – the detection of an exoplanet. After confirmation, it was celebrated in the astronomical community as a remarkable event, for it marked the first time an exoplanet – in this case, two – (**3**) _____ been discovered and confirmed as such.

Since then, more than 2,000 exoplanets (**4**) _____ been discovered. Scientists can actually detect atmospheric composition on these planets, which are anywhere (**5**) _____ four to almost 30,000 light-years away from Earth. As the planet passes in front of its star, they study the light that travels through its atmosphere; that is, if its parent star has (**6**) _____ blasted it away with solar winds. By studying the stellar spectrum, scientists can determine what elements are present. Naturally, they hope (**7**) _____ locate habitable worlds and, in the past, the near-Earth twins discovered (**8**) _____ make headline news. Still, space technology needs to progress much further in order to detect any meaningful signs of life anytime soon.

F Complete the second sentence so that it has a similar meaning to the first sentence, using the word given. Do not change the word given. You must use between three and eight words, including the word given.

1 Surely they will find life on other planets one day.

   bound

   One day, life _____.

2 I've got no plans to keep my ideas to myself during this meeting.

   shall

   During this meeting, I _____ to myself.

3 Jan and Vicky are about to have an argument, I fear.

   looming

   I'm afraid that an _____ between Jan and Vicky.

4 They are completely certain of the event's success.

   predict

   They _____ a success.

5 I was under the impression that he would pay for dinner.

   expected

   I _____ dinner.

6 Lisa meant to be rude when she asked Dan why he lied.

   trying

   While asking Dan about his lies, Lisa _____ polite.

Reading

A Read the *Exam Reminder*. What phrase in paragraph A of the *Exam Task* might help you to find the paragraph it follows?

_____

B Now complete the *Exam Task*.

Making the world a better place, one controversy at a time

In 2008, renegade Greenpeace activists Junichi Soto and Toru Suzuki seized a container of whale meat from a delivery depot in Aomori Prefecture, Japan. They believed that the meat was procured from government whaling research and was destined for sale in Japanese restaurants, a practice publicly condemned by the Japanese government. The confiscation sparked controversy for the government, which hastened a cover-up, characterising the meat as 'a souvenir' of the whalers. However, it was the fate of Soto and Suzuki which seemed particularly unjust. **1**

The pair didn't expect to be celebrated for uncovering the government scandal, but they were nonetheless surprised by the outcome of their actions. Ultimately the men were sentenced to one year in prison, which the judge mercifully suspended for three years. Unfazed, Sato expressed no regrets. 'Because of our case, many inside Japan are now aware of the whaling industry's kickbacks and embezzlement,' he remarked in an article he wrote for a British newspaper. **2**

In an attempt to bypass regulations, the government stipulated that the exploration could only be funded by sales of whale meat. But few had the wool pulled over their eyes and fleets of Greenpeace vessels showed up to confront the Japanese whaling ships. Dramatic scenes of ships a tenth the size of the government's fleet were broadcast in the news. Only years later did the Japanese government finally curtail their 'research', partly due to the Tokyo Two's exposé, and partly because of Greenpeace's involvement. **3**

Dubbed the 'Don't Make a Wave' campaign, the activists reached the US coastguard ship *Confidence*, which ordered them to retreat. The mission went ahead as planned, and although disheartened, the activists learnt that their endeavours had garnered worldwide attention. In realising that such extreme measures can have a global impact, the group began raising funds in order to campaign for environmentalism. Greenpeace was born. **4**

One such incident involved the Nazca lines in Peru. In an attempt to hang a banner protesting against climate change, activists damaged the UNESCO World Heritage site by walking on an area not open to the public and leaving visible footprints. The organisation was forced to issue an apology, one Peruvian officials were unwilling to accept. **5**

While it may hold firmly to perhaps upopular positions such as this, there is no doubt that Greenpeace strives to do good. Their mission centres around achieving a number of goals related to climate change, which tops their list, but also the protection of natural habitats, the fight against deforestation, nuclear disarmament and the promotion of sustainable agriculture. **6**

Aside from the corporations and government entities that they attack, Greenpeace has political opponents who try to slander or spy on them. Activists have claimed that their phones have been tapped and some have received threats on their lives. Although ultimately cleared of fraud, at one point its American subsidiary was accused of misreporting tax statements to the US government. **7**

What is certain is that they will continue to wage war against those who bring harm to the planet. But it's clear amongst Vancouver natives, in the city where the organisation was founded, that there exists great pride in its legacy. In the spirit of how it was founded – by a group of individuals – there are few places where you wouldn't meet a local who would make the spurious claim, 'Sure, I helped found Greenpeace.'

You are going to read an extract from a magazine article. Seven paragraphs have been removed from the extract. Choose from the paragraphs **A – H** the one which fits each gap (**1 – 7**). There is one extra paragraph which you do not need to use.

A Sloppy mistakes aside, the organisation has also come under criticism for its specific positions. In the case of genetically modified foods, a practice Greenpeace is vehemently against, 107 Nobel laureate scholars actually penned a letter to Greenpeace urging it to change its stance. They cited scientific evidence of the benefit of GM foods for farmers and consumers alike, and that not one single negative incident has resulted from the cultivation and consumption of such products.

B In fact, media outlets the world over have given Greenpeace an enormous amount of attention for its outlandish stunts. In one case, members produced a fake website for an oil company with articles about their inaugural drilling in the Arctic. The website fooled many people and was a blatant criticism of the oil company's practices, but critics were quick to pounce on its misleading premise.

C A report was filed in 2006 by a public watchdog suggesting that the company was exploiting its status as a non-profit organisation and falsifying its financial returns. Greenpeace was audited, but its books turned up clean. Subsequently, it was disclosed that the watchdog who blew the whistle had accepted a substantial donation from a gas and oil corporation, one of the entities Greenpeace fights against.

D The organisation was founded upon its ability to directly confront its opponents. Across the globe in Alaska some decades before the whaling incident, a group of Canadian activists sailed to Amchitka, an island in Alaska's Aleutian island chain. The US government intended to detonate an atomic bomb on the uninhabited island, ignoring warnings of seismic activity and the tsunamis it could trigger.

E Although they have cut back considerably on their presence in the Antarctic Ocean, Greenpeace's efforts to protect these majestic sea mammals stretches back decades. The organisation, which began in 1971, embarked in the mid-1980s on a mission to establish Antarctica as a world park. Although eventually successful, when Japan's whaling fleet appeared in the late 1980s under the guise of 'scientific research', it was clear a loophole had been exploited.

F Predictably, they have faced some criticism, as underscored by the Tokyo Two incident. Lawsuits have been filed against them for destroying fields of genetically modified crops and harassing fishing expeditions. They entered into a row with the Finnish government when they transported the trunk of a fallen tree to exhibitions to highlight the negative effects of logging there. And occasionally, the organisation's members make blunders that sully Greenpeace's image.

G Although the police launched an investigation into the whalers' actions, no charges were brought against them. Instead, they charged the activists and even mistreated them during their detention. The pair were denied legal representation and interrogated for a relentless 12 hours. The activists were even branded as terrorists and egregiously compared to a doomsday cult that released poisonous gas in a Tokyo underground station.

H As a testament to their work on these issues, Greenpeace successfully raised awareness of global warming in the 1990s. They clearly had an impact on the Japanese whaling industry, as the fleets have all but left Antarctica. Their revelations that major corporations were linked to tropical rainforest destruction resulted in policy changes in those companies. Their efforts in ridding the world of weapons of mass destruction and stopping the genetic modification of crops has so far been less successful.

Vocabulary

A Match these words to the description of the people.

apathetic   brutal   callous   corrupt   humane   merciful   prejudiced   tolerant

1 Maria is welcoming to all people in her community, regardless of race or age. _____

2 Mr Stiles is a hard-working public servant; that is, he works hard to do favours for members of the public who line his pockets with cash! _____

3 Jonathan believes refugees should be given shelter, have food, clothing and a livelihood, and be helped to seek asylum in another country. _____

4 Pol Pot, the former leader of present-day Cambodia, was a dictator responsible for the deaths of millions of Cambodians through forced labour and executions. _____

5 Although he had some good qualities, Marcus wasn't well-liked among his colleagues due to the cruel comments he would make about his customers. _____

6 Rather than sentence the youth to a term in a maximum-security prison, the judge took his circumstances into account and gave him a lighter punishment. _____

7 Barbara's aunt was always the cause of awkward moments because she would make comments to the rest of the family about how she didn't like foreigners. _____

8 Hank was a bit of a loner who kept to himself; he didn't seem to care much about others and would never get involved in his community to help out. _____

B Rewrite the words in bold as phrasal verbs.

1 The government will **abolish** the expensive application fee. _____
2 Wealthy nations must **confront** the issue of income disparity within their economies. _____
3 The success of this charity **depends on** the number and size of donations we can raise. _____
4 Due to a struggling economy, the organisation **reduced** its charitable expenditures. _____
5 The aid workers were pleased to see the success that **resulted from** their hard work. _____

C Choose the correct answers.

1 The workers _____ a protest over unpaid wages.
   a occupied   b made   c picketed   d staged
2 The charity director _____ funds for the disaster clean-up.
   a dispersed   b disbanded   c disbursed   d disposed
3 I simply cannot _____ the behaviour of a prejudiced, bigoted politician.
   a condone   b condemn   c condense   d conduct
4 Emergency services personnel _____ no effort in rescuing people inside the fallen building.
   a spent   b spared   c saved   d stopped
5 If I find out a company harms animals, I immediately _____ their products.
   a denounce   b suspend   c boycott   d refuse

D Complete the sentences with one word in each gap.

1 Despite severe weather conditions, some volunteers _____ to the rescue of the stranded motorist.
2 Several members of the community _____ a human chain so oil drillers couldn't get on to the land.
3 Jill put in a request for more funding, but after not receiving a reply, she assumed it had _____ on deaf ears.
4 Although slow-going in the beginning, some prominent individuals finally decided to _____ behind the cause.
5 These people suffering from devastating fires are members of our community and I'm not _____ my back on them.

E Read the *Exam Reminder* and complete the *Exam Task*.

Exam Task

For questions **1 – 8**, read the text below. Use the word given in capitals at the end of some of the lines to form a word that fits in the space in the same line.

Trusting the charities we give to

People contribute to charities because they find some
issues in society (**1**) _____. They are appalled by the   **TOLERATE**
disparity of wealth that has resulted in (**2**) _____ fellow   **POVERTY**
citizens and cannot abide the blatant (**3**) _____ for human   **REGARD**
life that governments are sometimes guilty of. But what happens
when a charity is accused of corruption, favouritism or the
(**4**) _____ of funds? Fortunately, there are watchdogs   **APPROPRIATE**
monitoring charities whose behaviour is somewhat (**5**) _____.   **REPUTE**
Endeavouring to warn the public about charities that
operate (**6**) _____, one such watchdog in the US   **LAW**
exposed four cancer charities, all of which were operated by one
man. He stood accused of spending donations on friends and
family members, rather than cancer patients, and submitting
(**7**) _____ financial records to tax authorities for decades.   **FRAUD**
What's encouraging, though, is that watchdogs and charity
evaluators are tracking and reporting on charities' activities
so that the public does not become (**8**) _____ of them.   **TRUST**

Exam Reminder

Forming negative words
- When you do word-formation tasks, remember that one or more gaps in the text may require a negative word.
- Remember that, while nouns and adjectives usually use prefixes to form negatives, different nouns and adjectives with the same root do not always use the same prefix.
- A variety of negative prefixes such as *un-, dis-, dys-, mis-, ill-, in-, im-* under- and *de-*, as well as the suffix *-less*, are used to form negative words.

Grammar

Uses of the passive; Transitive & intransitive verbs

A Rewrite the sentences that can be written in the passive. In which of those sentences is the agent optional and why? Why can't the other sentences be written in the passive?

1 The children had grown so much since Mary's last visit. _____
2 The starving travellers quickly devoured the plate of canapés. _____
3 The doctors are arriving on the 14th of September. _____
4 They laundered the money through a corrupt foreign bank. _____
5 Protesters lined the streets in anticipation of the prime minister. _____
6 Medical workers vaccinated 90 per cent of the residents in one day. _____

B Using word formation, change the words in bold so that the second sentence has the same meaning as the first sentence. You will use two to three words in each gap.

1 We must stop this **poor treatment of** animals immediately.
   These animals must not be _____ any longer.
2 I'm pleased that we **have been inundated generously** with donations.
   We have happily received a _____ donations.
3 The nation faced problems because it **relied heavily on** foreign oil.
   The nation's _____ foreign oil caused problems.
4 When questioned about the donation, she pretended that she **was ignorant**.
   She _____ when reporters asked her about the donation.

Avoiding the passive

C Rewrite the sentences using *under* and a noun.

1 The grant for the charity is being reviewed.
   _____

2 They are constructing a new nursery.
   _____

3 The burglar has been arrested.
   _____

4 Carol is suspected of being the thief.
   _____

5 There is an attack on the fort.
   _____

Passive Causative with *get* & *have*

D Complete the text with a causative form of the words in brackets. More than one answer may be possible.

Those who lose everything, those who sacrifice to help

Charity groups work in a multitude of ways to improve people's lives. For those who
(1) _____ (**destroy their homes**) by floods, earthquakes and other natural disasters, getting a new home built means the world. When a community **(2)** _____ (**strike their farmland**) by drought that results in starvation, they are going to be reliant on the staples given to them by these charities.

In one such case in 2002, the city of Goma, Congo **(3)** _____ (**consume a tenth of its buildings**) by lava from a volcanic eruption. Roads were rendered impassable, blocking help from reaching residents, but aid workers, desperate to deliver supplies, **(4)** _____ (**bulldoze a route**) and around two weeks later, residents **(5)** _____ (**deliver aid**) on a regular basis.

Luckily, there is a wide spectrum of professionals willing to freely donate their services. Many impoverished world citizens **(6)** _____ (**check health currently**) by highly-skilled doctors and nurses who have decided to sacrifice their time and comfort for a worthy cause.

E Read the *Exam Reminder* and complete the *Exam Task*.

Exam Task

For questions **1 – 5**, complete the second sentence so that it has a similar meaning to the first sentence, using the word given. **Do not change the word given.** You must use between **three** and **eight** words, including the word given.

1 They have been closely examining the charity's activities lately.
scrutiny
The activities _____ lately.

2 The aid workers are still constructing the new school.
got
The aid _____ yet.

3 The beachgoers ran to high ground when they saw the tsunami.
had
The tsunami _____ high ground.

4 The authorities believe there will not be any disturbances at the protest.
expected
The protest _____ peaceful.

5 They are currently occupying a public building.
under
A public building _____ at the moment.

Listening

A Read the *Exam Reminder*. What words in the *Exam Task* answer choices might indicate a need to listen for opinions?

B 3.1 ▷❙❙ Listen and complete the *Exam Task*.

_____

Exam Task

You will hear eight short conversations. From the three answer choices, select the answer which means the same as what you hear or is true based upon what you hear.

1 a Mark has been passionate about things lately.
  b The woman thinks Mark should take care of his responsibilities.
  c The man is going to assist Mark in moving house.

2 a The protestors have blocked roads.
  b The man thinks the protestors are a nuisance.
  c The woman explains the situation with the roads.

3 a The man believes people should be wary of striking.
  b The woman essentially agrees with the man.
  c The man would like to get higher wages in his job.

4 a The man believes vehicle possession is overrated.
  b The woman expresses a concern about strict laws.
  c The woman thinks lives could be saved by the law.

5 a The woman feels sorry for Shelley.
  b Shelley has difficulty relating to others' feelings.
  c Neither the man nor the woman like Shelley.

6 a The system was installed subsequent to the burglary.
  b The man installed the alarm system himself.
  c The alarm system was installed prior to the burglary.

7 a The woman believes the toxic waste issue is being purposefully ignored.
  b The government is taking a head-on approach to the clean-up.
  c The woman thinks the government is unaware of the problem.

8 a The man appreciates the woman's daughter's position.
  b The woman expresses concern over her daughter's views.
  c The man hopes the woman admonished her daughter.

C 3.2 ▷❙❙ Listen again and check your answers.

Writing: an article (1)

A Complete the titles with a phrase that makes them more engaging for readers. Why is one choice better than the other?

1 How to save / I saved a forest
2 Less pollution is the only way forward / solution
3 Giving a helping hand to a dog / man's best friend
4 Don't let our future go up in smoke / get polluted
5 Helping those who had to leave / forced to flee
6 There's no excuse for animal abuse / hurting animals

Learning Reminder

Engaging your reader
- Articles are meant to be informative, but they are most successful when they have captured the reader's attention.
- Give your article a title that describes your focus but also sparks interest.
- You can use a rhetorical question in the introductory paragraph to make the reader want to read the article in order to find out the answer.
- Use humour, relatable examples and thought-provoking quotes to entertain and enlighten readers, and use a semi-formal, conversational writing style.

B Explain the common quotes in your own words.

1 'Society can be judged by how it treats animals.'

_____

2 'Actions speak louder than words.'

_____

3 'Charity begins at home, but should not end there.'

_____

4 'The best way to predict the future is to create it.'

_____

C Read the paragraphs from longer articles. For each paragraph, choose a title from exercise A that would be appropriate for the whole article, complete the gap with a quote from exercise B and rewrite the underlined sentence as a rhetorical question.

1 Article title: _____

Each year, millions of people are displaced due to conflict in their home country. Those of us who live in more politically stable countries and have either time or money to spare must do something to help. As the saying goes, '_____' These people are going through the worst times in their lives and they deserve help from those who are in a position to do so. <u>After all, the thought of having to leave your home is unimaginable indeed.</u>

2 Article title: _____

During a recent camping trip with my family, I witnessed some disturbing images – discarded belongings strewn about the ground, rubbish blocking a part of a small river and a most uninviting stench. This came after hearing that the government would be making more of a commitment to find solutions to environmental issues. Clearly, the old adage '_____' seems to apply to this situation. I knew I had to do something when I realised that <u>if the natural world was completely ruined, life would be unimaginable.</u>

3 Article title: _____

There's an area of my town we like to refer to as No Man's Land. It's an industrial area that's very ugly, the air around it is very polluted and the government has more or less forgotten about it. My classmates and I recently decided to do something about this blighted area. You know what they say, '_____' So I'm going to tell you what we accomplished in order to turn this area around in case it happens to you because, let's face it, <u>you wouldn't like having to live in a place as polluted as this.</u>

D Read and complete the *Exam Task* below. Don't forget to use the *Useful Expressions* on page 47 of your Student's Book.

Exam Task

You have seen an editor's appeal in a magazine for articles on caring for stray animals. You decide to write an article in which you describe an animal shelter that you've visited, explain how you help them out and say why it is important for your community.

Write your **article** in 280–320 words.

▶) Writing Reference p. 207 in Student's Book

Reading

A Read the *Exam Reminder*. Which options in the *Exam Task* questions seem to contain truths?

_____

B Now complete the *Exam Task*.

Forging a better social bond

Findings from studies on social connections reveal a broad spectrum of truths: that men and women need one another – as friends, as romantic partners, as cooperative colleagues, and so forth. Studies also reveal the struggles we face as a society in our efforts to forge meaningful bonds, why some people encounter obstacles, and what behaviours, habits, processes and in some cases medication can rev up our social engines. A father cuddling his newborn baby, lunch with a long-standing, respected co-worker who embraces your ideas and hugging a beloved relative after being apart for some time can all release a hormone from a very small part of our brain.

This hormone, oxytocin, which originates from the pituitary gland, a pea-sized gland situated at the base of our brain, has in medical research been long associated with childbirth. It induces labour and has been used as such in hospitals for decades. While naturally produced, it has been replicated in laboratories and it has been deemed safe for use by the medical community. Its discovery as a 'cuddle hormone', which it is oft-called due to its ability to make people more sociable, has thrust it into the spotlight as a way of healing our – what some sociologists might hypothesise – increasingly disconnected society.

Commercially available, oxytocin poses no known physical risks or causes any adverse changes in cognitive function. Clinical trials show people who have had the hormone administered to their bloodstream display warm, affectionate behaviour with loved ones, strengthening their already-established bonds. Consumers can purchase nasal sprays and atomisers manufactured with traces of oxytocin, albeit for a rather exorbitant price, and its molecular likeness has even been imprinted on pillows, coffee mugs and T-shirts, as evidence of its ascendancy in our collective consciousness as a love-inducing hormone. Missing, though, are much-needed stamps of approval from national food and drug administrations, but aside from cost, branding or regulatory issues, its use is hampered by the peculiar effect it has on negative bonds.

Research shows the specific effect oxytocin has relates to the type of bond a person has with another. It amplifies whatever bond is present; that is to say, close bonds are strengthened, but if a person has antagonistic feelings towards someone else, they become more unfriendly and incompatible. An example often cited in research is its effect on males and their relationships with their parents, specifically their mother. The hormone elicited more praise from men who got on well with their mums, and more criticism in cases where mum and son regularly clashed. Further corroboration of this effect could be seen in individuals who, after inhaling the hormone, were more likely to become more amiable with established friends; concerning outsiders, however, the hormone effectively had an opposite, repelling effect.

One of the most pressing problems facing society today is the increasing lack of bonds that men and women have with outsiders, such as foreigners or people of differing faiths, or perhaps even people who are simply outside one's inner circle of friends. We can point the finger at various culprits for this reality: social media, which has relegated us to computer screens, or xenophobia, due to the increase, whether perceived or real, of refugees and foreigners coming to our country. They are viewed as nothing more than job-takers or freeloaders, even though statistical information suggests otherwise.

In search of a panacea for these ills, the use of oxytocin could almost be viewed as a case of 'be careful what you wish for' were its undesirable effects worse. But we don't really need to go back to the drawing board – more holistic methods of forming bonds, such as seeking out company with like-minded individuals, go further than scientific intervention. The true challenge is encouraging people to exploit those methods. While it's inarguably easier to go online and sift through news feeds, our bonds are breaking as a result. People still need the human touch, smiles, the favours we do for one another, such as make a cup of tea for someone, or even the shopping trips we take with each together. A famous person once said, 'Life was much easier when Apple and Blackberry were just fruits.' Easier, and perhaps more rewarding, too.

You are going to read an article about social bonding. For questions **1 – 6**, choose the answer (**a**, **b**, **c** or **d**) which you think fits best according to the text.

1 How would you characterise the author's discussion of social bonding in the first paragraph?

a He treats the subject matter with a very narrow point of view.

b He speaks broadly about social connections and doesn't give specifics.

c He leads up to its connection with a naturally produced substance.

d He highlights the struggles that some people have with forming bonds.

2 What does the author suggest is the belief of people who study social connections?

a The connections people have today exhibit many positive attributes.

b Secrets to social bonding may exist in treatments used for childbirth.

c We might have to resort to unorthodox forms of treatment to fix society.

d There may be cause for alarm due to how society is now developing.

3 The author believes that oxytocin's image on things that can be bought

a was brought about by its verifiable effectiveness.

b is a testament to its perceived impact on society.

c demonstrates the power of horde mentality.

d means it should be regulated by authorities.

4 What is the author's purpose in mentioning the study in paragraph 4?

a to inform people of conclusive clinical evidence

b to temper the suggestion that oxytocin is a cure-all

c to show flaws in research that negate previous understanding

d to present another point of view about the application of oxytocin

5 Why does the author lump together social media and a fear of foreigners?

a Studies indicate the two have a connection.

b Both seem to be causing a certain type of ill in society.

c Both include people with a lack of knowledge of the world.

d Because the author has a negative view of both of these things.

6 What can be concluded about the author's feelings about oxytocin?

a Its commercial use was never really necessary in the first place.

b There's no real harm in conducting further studies.

c A search for a better alternative must ensue.

d It should only ever be used by certain people.

Vocabulary

A **Complete the sentences with these words.**

choir   diaspora   dynasty   flock   lobby   pack   throng   troupe

1 The anti-smoking _____ was successful in getting the ban passed.

2 A _____ of people began to gather in the arena, waiting for the performance.

3 The Ming _____ is one of the most famous ruling families in China's history.

4 As Beth went over to greet Nathan in the square, she disturbed a _____ of pigeons.

5 The Gilberts make up a travelling _____ of violin players.

6 During the Greek _____ in the 1960s, many settled in Queens in New York.

7 Be careful that you don't come across a _____ of wolves in the vast forest.

8 Josh sang in the church _____ and went on to become a huge YouTube sensation.

B **Each sentence has one incorrect word or phrase. Cross it out and write the correct word or phrase.**

1 Gina isn't in a one-side relationship; she's the most selfless person I know. _____

2 In a remarkable chain of events, Henry found his long-gone twin sister on Facebook after being apart for years. _____

3 Jane and her cousin lived next door to each other and were the most of friends. _____

4 That over a billion and a half people are on Facebook is a brain-boggling fact. _____

5 Paul woke up on the incorrect side of the bed this morning and it shows in his mood. _____

6 Mary and Sue spent nearly every weekend together as teenagers; they were as dense as thieves. _____

7 They hit it off as friends, but after a nasty argument early on, their friendship proved to be quick-lived. _____

8 According to the theory of six levels of separation, we're all just six contacts away from everyone else. _____

C Read the blog and circle the correct words.

25th May Ignore Request

I don't mean to be cynical or (**1**) shrink / detract from the value of social media; honestly, I adore catching (**2**) over / up with my friends on Facebook and seeing what topics are (**3**) overpowering / dominating my news feed. But occasionally, I get a friend request from a blast from the past – someone wanting to (**4**) keep / get in touch with me after years of no contact, which is what happened today. Yeah, I was sort of friends with her back then. I think we (**5**) paired / met up maybe half a dozen times during school. Her friend request isn't even a genuine attempt to touch (**6**) base / root; she just wants to brag about her life! I wish her all the best, but I'm not interested in rekindling an (**7**) on-and-off / in-and-out friendship that neither of us were really into in the first place. What's important is that you never (**8**) lose / miss touch with the people you really care about in life.

D Complete the sentences with the correct form of the words in bold.

1   You shouldn't have washed this shirt in hot water; I'm afraid it's suffered from _____.   **SHRINK**

2   Saying you have a lot of friends but you don't like people is a rather _____ statement.   **CONTRADICT**

3   Sean has a group of friends he plays online games with, but none of them live in close _____ to him.   **PROXIMATE**

4   If few foreigners live in a particular country, one might characterise the society as being quite _____.   **HOMOGENISE**

5   Although the network of companies didn't need one another to survive, their close _____ allowed them to thrive.   **DEPEND**

6   The main effect of _____ is that our world has become much smaller, but arguably more efficient.   **GLOBAL**

7   When wireless internet _____ was established in the Himalayas, it had truly reached the far corners of the globe.   **CONNECT**

8   Go ahead and accuse me of being _____, but sometimes I'd like to be on a deserted island with no one around to disturb me!   **SOCIAL**

E Read the *Exam Reminder* and complete the *Exam Task*.

Exam Task

Choose the word or phrase that best completes the sentence.

1   The journalists' _____ held a meeting to discuss industry-related issues.
    a band   b crew
    c union   d cabinet

2   Matt dumped Elisabeth on Facebook; they're not even on _____ terms.
    a speaking   b talking
    c listening   d hearing

3   After the disastrous televised interview, the topic was _____ on social media.
    a raging   b moving
    c trending   d buzzing

4   When everyone starts to dress alike, it tends to _____ society.
    a diversify   b homogenise
    c coalesce   d faction

5   Let me know of any pertinent developments; keep me in the _____.
    a sphere   b ring
    c circle   d loop

Exam Reminder

Dealing with synonymous vocabulary

• Questions that have answer choices with similar meanings often require you to complete a set phrase or collocation, such as *kill* time, as opposed to *slaughter*, *slay* or *murder* time.

• When the gap doesn't complete a set phrase, you must understand the differences in meaning between the words. For example, the words *harvest* and *cultivate* go with *crops*, but the former means 'to gather' and the latter 'to grow'.

• Consider the meaning of the whole sentence and try all options before making your choice.

6   It was a pleasure to make your _____, Mr Shephard.
    a friendship   b acquaintance
    c relationship   d contact

7   They called the fire _____ as soon as they saw smoke.
    a squad   b mob
    c platoon   d brigade

8   Don't _____ Jason in the photo when you upload it to Instagram – you know he hates having any personal information online.
    a avatar   b tag
    c join   d follow

Grammar

Modal Verbs; Past Tense Modals; Negative forms; *Need & Dare*

A Write sentences using modals according to the prompts. More than one answer may be possible.

1 she / not locate / her friend's profile / Twitter (**past ability**)

_____

2 they / say / thanks / when / they / leave / party (**past action, criticism**)

_____

3 he / register / multiple accounts / same site (**past action, probability**)

_____

4 we / send / texts / while / drive / vehicle (**present prohibition**)

_____

5 we / not invite / the O'Hares / wedding? (**present advice**)

_____

6 I / not create / online profile / I / prefer / anonymity (**present refusal**)

_____

B Complete the dialogues with the correct form of these words and a modal verb. More than one answer may be possible.

delete   move   post   recognise   spend   upload

1 'It was nice of Betty and Sam to wave at me when they saw me.'
'Wait … they _____ you. I'm one hundred per cent sure you've never met!'

2 'I've got rid of all our emails to each other, so they can't be read.'
'You _____ them. No one can access your account anyway.'

3 'I saw all your photos from your shopping spree with Ellen.'
'Oh, she _____ those. I look terrible in them!'

4 'What shocked you most about the study?'
'That the average university student _____ eight to ten hours a day using their mobiles.'

5 'Please submit your CV as an email attachment when you can.'
'_____ it in the mail as well? My internet connection is sometimes spotty.'

C Complete the sentences with *dare* or *need* and the correct form of the verbs in brackets. More than one answer may be possible.

1 _____ (**mention**) that you broke her phone – she'll be livid!

2 He _____ (**publish**) photos of the royal family – they will sue.

3 They've been banned from Facebook – _____ (**say**) more?

4 You _____ (**apologise**) for getting involved in the argument – it's not your fault.

5 They _____ (**buy**) me a new laptop – it's quite nice, but I could have fixed my old one.

D Choose the correct answers.

1 'Can't I create a fake online profile?'
'No, you _____.'
  a don't have to   **b** mustn't   **c** won't

2 'Why is Monica so angry with me?'
'You _____ have made your private conversations public.'
  a should   **b** mustn't   **c** shouldn't

3 Did Mark write in his blog that he hates all his classmates? That _____ be correct!
  a can   **b** can't   **c** might not

4 The invitation isn't in my inbox, so she _____ have sent it yet.
  a needn't   **b** oughtn't   **c** might not

E Read the *Exam Reminder* and complete the *Exam Task*.

Exam Task

For questions **1 – 8**, read the text below and think of the word which best fits each space. Use only **one** word in each space.

Kick the online bully in you

A recent study showed that once children reach the age where they're able to use the internet and have a social media account, around 50 per cent **(1)** _____ go on to do some kind of online bullying. We might think that statistic **(2)** _____ be true, but it's roughly equal to the percentage of children who claim to have been bullied. Online bullies need **(3)** _____ necessarily be juvenile delinquents; most are just blithely unaware of how hurtful their remarks can be. If they were brought up correctly by their parents, they certainly **(4)** _____ to know better than to do it, but often it takes a realisation about the feelings of others to change their conduct. For that to happen, the bully **(5)** _____ experience the reaction of the bullied first-hand. With the anonymity provided by the internet, bullies **(6)** _____ often easily get away with their taunts. But what **(7)** _____ happen to children who get caught bullying – have their accounts frozen or get banned from using the internet? The latter would **(8)** _____ to be up to parents, but unfortunately they're sometimes the source of the problem in the first place.

Listening

A Read the *Exam Reminder*. What do you think you would hear after a speaker said 'in fact'?

_____

B 4.1 ▶|| Listen and complete the *Exam Task*.

Exam Task

You will hear part of a discussion between two research assistants, Mike Garner and Annabelle Huckabee, who are talking about relationships people have online and in real life. For questions **1 – 5**, choose the answer (**a**, **b**, **c** or **d**) which best fits according to what you hear.

1 What point is made about Dunbar's number?
  a The number can predict the number of online friends a person will have.
  b Dunbar's number has no connection whatsoever to the number of online friends a person has.
  c While thus far unproven, it could apply to the number of online friends a person can have.
  d More understanding of Dunbar's number is needed for the research study.

2 Annabelle was surprised to learn that
  a a person could have upwards of 120 online friends.
  b the more meaningful friendships exist online, rather than in real life.
  c removing barriers to making friends results in making a great number of friends.
  d the brain limits the number of friends people can have.

3 What view is stated about human contact?
  a It is the single most important factor in making friends.
  b A lack of it results in fewer friends, real or online.

  c An online friendship can only be so meaningful without it.
  d It could discourage a friend from being too revealing.

4 As to why people make friends online, Mike and Annabelle differ regarding
  a the motivating force behind it.
  b people's end goals.
  c the quality of friendships found.
  d the satisfaction they receive.

5 What conclusion do both researchers arrive at concerning online usage?
  a We must better learn how to unlock its potential.
  b Learning our limits is the key to mastering it.
  c Its negative aspects will always challenge us.
  d People must focus more on real life and avoid the online one.

C 4.2 ▶|| Listen again and check your answers.

Writing: a letter (1)

A **Match the paragraphs to the target audiences.**

1 A good crowdfunding campaign takes organisation, and I would like to advertise it through social media, in hopes that more community members will donate. I would also like your office to endorse the campaign publicly, as that will help us reach our goals. ☐

2 I am writing in response to the ban on mobile phone use that the board has imposed on educational institutions. Hindering our ability to communicate with one another only leads to isolation. What it achieves is it makes individuals resent the very place where they are supposed to learn. ☐

3 Exchanging pleasantries with our neighbours is about as far as most people go in getting to know one another these days. It's this lack of contact that I have witnessed in our neighbourhood, so I am taking it upon myself to organise a meet-and-greet at our town hall this coming Saturday. ☐

4 My main argument against social media is that, if misused, it can harm a person's reputation and even result in a loss of friends or a job. Had I known of the dangers, I might not have ever opened an account. As such, I would like to share my advice for staying out of harm's way. ☐

   a a magazine editor   **b** a local government official
   c a headmaster   **d** community members

Learning Reminder

Following letter-writing conventions

- Begin and end your letter with a polite greeting and closing, and remember to open with your reason for writing and conclude your letter appropriately.
- Keep your target audience in mind: letters to publications will likely include a personal experience, whereas letters to public officials will include plans, facts and details.
- Keep the style formal throughout.

B **Look at the paragraphs in exercise A again and complete the tasks below. Some phrases may need more than one type of mark.**

1 <u>Underline</u> cleft sentences.
2 (Circle) inversions and gerund clauses.
3 Tick (✓) persuasive ideas.
4 Star (*) future plans.

C **Read the partial *Exam Task* rubrics. Using these ideas, the prompt for each task and sentence types from exercise B, write appropriate paragraphs. Then answer the questions.**

careful consideration   cooperation   increased interaction   mutual trust   permanent record
privacy issues   ruined reputation   shared ideas

1 *... a letter in response to an article on how to protect yourself online ...*
Personally, I protect myself online simply because
_____
_____
_____
_____
_____

2 *... a letter on a proposal to raise money for a new community centre ...*
Going forward, _____
_____
_____
_____
_____

- To whom would you write these letters?
- Which would benefit from a plan and which from an experience?

- Under which part of the letter plan on page 61 of your Student's Book would your paragraphs fall?

D **Read and complete the *Exam Task* below. Don't forget to use the *Useful Expressions* on page 61 of your Student's Book.**

Exam Task

Some people in your community want to renovate a run-down community theatre. You decide to send a letter to the mayor to get his support for a crowdfunding campaign. Briefly describe why you're starting the campaign, explain how you plan to organise it and how the mayor can contribute, and say how the campaign and the project will impact the community.

Write your **letter** in 280–320 words.

🔄 Writing Reference p. 209 in Student's Book

Vocabulary

A   **Choose the correct answers.**

1 There are still native _____ of people that have never had contact with the developed world.

  a packs   **b** mobs

  c tribes   **d** races

2 The employees are _____ a rally in the city centre to demand higher wages.

  a making   **b** performing

  c staging   **d** presenting

3 Having lost her home, Lucy got _____ a gang of people who hang around causing trouble.

  a in with   **b** up to

  c on with   **d** by on

4 Although usually quite compassionate, the receptionist made a _____ remark that took her colleagues by surprise.

  a crooked   **b** cautious

  c corrupt   **d** callous

5 Once Steven and Jill starting earning good salaries, they moved to a(n) _____ suburb.

  a flourishing   **b** plush

  c affluent   **d** emergent

6 I tried to get the singer's autograph, but I couldn't get past her massive _____.

  a horde   **b** posse

  c entourage   **d** cast

7 Pavlos, having lived in Greece all his life, decided to _____ to the UK for a change.

  a immigrate   **b** emigrate

  c migrate   **d** evacuate

8 I barely know Harold; he's just a casual _____ who I met through a friend.

  a friendship   **b** relationship

  c association   **d** acquaintance

9 Julie felt unfairly _____ when she spoke out against a company proposal and the entire staff team turned against her.

  a prosecuted   **b** persecuted

  c oppressed   **d** suppressed

10 It would be considered a massive _____ on democracy if we couldn't vote for a president.

  a raid   **b** assault

  c strike   **d** battery

11 Lisa made a _____ over government plans to build on a national park.

  a break   **b** mess

  c fuss   **d** noise

12 I've been trying Ralph all day, but his phone must be off because I can't get _____ of him.

  a catch   **b** grasp

  c grip   **d** hold

13 The _____ ruler was mourned by the whole country on his passing.

  a benevolent   **b** violent

  c brutal   **d** beneficial

14 If we did _____ high fees for residence cards, less fortunate immigrants could rightfully obtain legal residency.

  a with   **b** without

  c away with   **d** over

15 Every time I return to my home town, I always _____ base with a few close friends.

  a tap   **b** knock

  c pat   **d** touch

16 Workers _____ a protest at the plant because of unsafe conditions.

  a formed   **b** mounted

  c occupied   **d** boycotted

17 Employees at the factory were miserable due to being consistently _____.

  a underpaid   **b** prepaid

  c overpaid   **d** unpaid

18 Jeff's been a staunch supporter of mine for years and I can't _____ my back on him now.

  a spin   **b** roll

  c twist   **d** turn

19 Once a major politician endorsed the young man's candidacy, everyone _____ on the bandwagon and started supporting him, too.

  a walked   **b** stepped

  c jumped   **d** climbed

20 When the police arrived, the crowd outside the town hall quickly _____.

  a dispensed   **b** disbursed

  c dispersed   **d** disbanded

Grammar

B Choose the correct answers.

1 The report says that the average university graduate _____ less than their parents throughout their career.
   - **a** would earn
   - **b** earned
   - **c** earns
   - **d** will earn

2 The building _____ dozens of protesters.
   - **a** occupied
   - **b** was occupied with
   - **c** was occupied by
   - **d** was occupied

3 You _____ park directly in front of the building entrance; they'll tow away your car.
   - **a** might not
   - **b** needn't
   - **c** don't
   - **d** mustn't

4 In protest at killing animals for their fur, a woman wearing a fur coat _____ red paint.
   - **a** got covered with
   - **b** get covered
   - **c** covered with
   - **d** to got covered

5 Although she was hard-working and honest, her actions as a diplomat were _____ scrutiny.
   - **a** out of
   - **b** beneath
   - **c** under
   - **d** below

6 We _____ the vents cleaned today because of a build-up of dust and mould.
   - **a** get
   - **b** are cleaning
   - **c** have
   - **d** are having

7 Her tireless efforts as a politician led to child labour _____.
   - **a** banned
   - **b** being banned
   - **c** ban
   - **d** was banned

8 Our neighbours _____ twice by the time we moved out of the neighbourhood.
   - **a** had their home burgled
   - **b** burgled their home
   - **c** got their home burgled
   - **d** have their home burgled

9 It's getting late; _____ start heading home?
   - **a** we had better
   - **b** hadn't we better
   - **c** we hadn't better
   - **d** had we better

10 I'm not fully aware of her schedule, but she ____ be going to Frankfurt on Friday.
   - **a** may
   - **b** must
   - **c** should
   - **d** can

11 I just charged my mobile phone – the battery ____ have died already!
   - **a** oughtn't
   - **b** needn't
   - **c** can't
   - **d** mustn't

12 You ____ a table for us, as I had already done it.
   - **a** mustn't book
   - **b** needn't book
   - **c** mustn't have booked
   - **d** needn't have booked

13 That file has sensitive information in it; ____ look through it!
   - **a** daren't
   - **b** dare
   - **c** do dare not
   - **d** don't you dare

14 Mary's one tough cookie; you ____ worried about hurting her feelings.
   - **a** ought be
   - **b** ought to be
   - **c** oughtn't be
   - **d** oughtn't to be

15 Johnny ____ been a champion skier, but a bad accident crushed his dream.
   - **a** needn't have
   - **b** shouldn't have
   - **c** could've
   - **d** must have

16 Darren's been accused of blaming others for his mistakes … ____ more?
   - **a** I need to say
   - **b** need I say
   - **c** need I to say
   - **d** need say I

17 I'm sure Lisa ____ to the charity because she's quite mean with money.
   - **a** would have given
   - **b** would give
   - **c** will have given
   - **d** won't give

18 You can't enter the boardroom now; the meeting is ____ progress.
   - **a** by
   - **b** on
   - **c** under
   - **d** in

19 The punishing heat ____ trapped indoors around midday.
   - **a** residents got
   - **b** residents had
   - **c** got residents
   - **d** had residents

20 The teacher ____ to search for the answer in their books.
   - **a** got the children
   - **b** had the children
   - **c** made the children
   - **d** has the children

Use of English

C Read the text below and decide which answer (a, b, c or d) best fits each gap.

The fight for women's rights

Lowell, Massachusetts is not a particularly (**1**) _____ place; it's a medium-sized town of about 100,000 citizens, most of whom have average incomes and live comfortable lives. But it serves as a turning point in the history of women's rights, as the women there fought against the (**2**) _____ conditions they endured at the city's textile mills in the 1800s. Almost 8,000 women – some as young as 13 – were employed at the mills that (**3**) _____ the industrial landscape of Lowell at the time. Employment gave these 'Mill Girls' a certain kind of independence for the first time in their lives, because before then, their husbands did not (**4**) _____ their wives or daughters working outside the home.

But before this story begins to sound like a tale of employer (**5**) _____, it is important to point out that employers hired the women at half the wages of the men, proving that there was nothing truly kind in their actions. They thought they could (**6**) _____ away with it, but in an ironic twist, the women, with their new-found sense of empowerment, (**7**) _____ a strike against their employers. Some very positive developments came (**8**) _____ the resistance; employers had to cave in to their demands and the women were offered better wages and working conditions.

1	**a** effective	**b** instrumental	**c** affluent	**d** impoverished
2	**a** oppressive	**b** domineering	**c** stifling	**d** overwhelming
3	**a** detracted	**b** distracted	**c** dominated	**d** diversified
4	**a** condemn	**b** contain	**c** condone	**d** confine
5	**a** benevolence	**b** justice	**c** equality	**d** mercy
6	**a** stay	**b** run	**c** do	**d** get
7	**a** occupied	**b** mounted	**c** formed	**d** pickets
8	**a** away with	**b** up to	**c** down on	**d** out of

D Read the text below and think of the word which best fits each gap. Use only one word in each gap.

A new report states that two-thirds of the world's wildlife (**1**) _____ definitely be lost in just a few short years unless urgent action (**2**) _____ taken to reverse the trend. While much awareness has been raised about habitat loss, many government officials are still (**3**) _____ their heads in the sand over the issue, choosing to ignore this serious problem rather than (**4**) _____ up to the facts. This has resulted in many forests, seas and other natural areas (**5**) _____ decimated at an alarming rate. Scientists characterise this loss of wildlife as nothing less than a mass extinction – the sixth such one in the planet's existence, and they say that mankind had (**6**) _____ get a handle on the situation before it gets out of control. A loss of habitat also means a loss of resources such as fresh water, which would in turn spark conflicts amongst populations. But this stark future need (**7**) _____ come to pass, as some wildlife, such as tigers and pandas, has rebounded, demonstrating that humans can have a positive impact on the fate of the planet. What people the world over must do is band (**8**) _____ and pressure governments to prevent habitat destruction, for the sake of humanity and animals alike.

E Complete the text with the correct form of the words in bold.

No time for work at work?

One could easily guess that the biggest (1) _____ in the workplace has something to do with the internet. In fact, it has become common to think of surfing the net at work as (2) _____ with shirking work responsibilities. But if it's not the net, then it's mobile phone use, gossiping, emails, snack breaks, meetings – all with the common thread of being (3) _____, if not social, in nature. So frequent are interruptions that many employees (4) _____ let their work slide and ultimately it suffers. Before they know it, they're having to rush to complete reports with a (5) _____ for quality. Numerous workplaces have previously allowed about an hour per day for workers to use the internet, but they are now becoming more (6) _____ of the practice. Restricting access may be the only way forward if a lack of productivity results in companies suffering (7) _____ damage due to a dramatic (8) _____ of revenue.

DISTRACT

ANALOGY

RECREATE
CONSCIOUS

REGARD

TOLERANT

REPAIR
SHRINK

F Complete the second sentence so that it has a similar meaning to the first sentence, using the word given. Do not change the word given. You must use between three and eight words, including the word given.

1 The board were reviewing the applications at that time.
   under
   At that time, the applications _____ board.

2 He was criticised for yelling at his students by the head teacher.
   yelled
   The head teacher believed that _____ at his student.

3 The poor ratings are the reason for the cancellation of the programme.
   being
   The _____ is due to poor ratings.

4 The charity is handling the repainting of their house.
   getting
   They _____ charity.

5 My advice is to avoid mentioning the incident that happened at school.
   dare
   If I were you, I _____ at school.

6 It's not possible that they paid for that mansion in cash.
   have
   They _____ that mansion in cash.

Reading

A Read the *Exam Reminder*. What phrases in the *Exam Task* paragraphs would you underline to help you answer the questions?

_____

B Now complete the *Exam Task*.

Determination is anything but frozen

For millennia, mankind has used sculpture to represent many things: devotion to faith, the aggrandisement of humanity or for merely decorative purposes. One thing in almost all cases that remains true about sculpture is its permanence. **1**

It is a testament to man's ability to create things for the sake of creating. Never mind how long it lasts or how much effort went into the creation of it. It was there, it existed for a short while and now it's gone, only to live on as a memory, as a catalogued experience. In a world so conditioned to aspire to durability, it is a challenging feat to create something that's quite the opposite. **2**

For the ice hotels of Scandinavia, that's almost exactly what happens. They are a miraculous feat, these hotels: of course, the walls are made of blocks of ice, but so is much of the furniture, including the seating that makes up the bars and restaurants. Even the drinks are served in glasses made of ice. **3**

The construction of large ice structures such as these is not a new concept. In the 18th century, Empress Anna Ivanovna commissioned an ice palace to be constructed in honour of Russia's defeat of Ottoman forces. This frozen palace marked the first such structure of its kind – the predecessor of the ice structures created today. **4**

Such a massive structure was obviously built to demonstrate a sense of pride in man and country. Other such structures were later erected in a smattering of American and Canadian cities, which essentially served as a kind of symbol of the arrival of affluence to these newer nations. It has since become a tradition in cities such as Quebec City and St Paul to erect structures every so often. **5**

Despite much fanfare, it was a commercial flop and city officials decided not to invest in such a venture again. It was simply too costly to build a structure that would only last for three months. The site was eventually razed and homes were built on it. **6**

An even deeper connection could be drawn between the ephemeral nature of ice sculptures and our experience of life, which is also temporary. Mankind toils through blood, sweat and tears to strive for excellence, which, like an ice sculpture, does not last forever. In a sense, an ice sculpture represents a sliver of what we face in life. **7**

The latter is certainly proof that mankind's determination knows no bounds, nor does it consider the longevity of a creation. Just like the sandcastles we create as children, which crumble away as the sea laps at their bases, so do the ice sculptures reaching several storeys in height become meaningless puddles under the warming sun.

You are going to read an extract from a magazine article. Seven paragraphs have been removed from the extract. Choose from the paragraphs **A – H** the one which fits each gap (**1 – 7**). There is one extra paragraph which you do not need to use.

A Our standard ideals about creation can take a bit of letting go of. For most people, if they had spent so much time and energy building a structure, they would want it to remain, to be enjoyed by others over and over again. To see something like this melt away into nothingness flies in the face of conventional wisdom.

B Even some smaller municipalities, such as Saranac Lake, New York, construct ice castles almost on an annual basis in a tradition that goes back decades. In the late 1800s, a poor mining town in Colorado constructed a giant ice castle to generate income from tourism. A dazzling sight, its walls were bluish-white and visitors could entertain themselves on an adjacent ice-skating rink and a toboggan slide.

C But for all the ice sculptors out there, that depressing thought does not discourage them from their craft. They teach us that no circumstance should inhibit us from creating, from achieving our dreams. Equipped with hammers, razor-sharp chisels, even chainsaws, they can create something as simple as a centrepiece for a cruise liner buffet or as grandiose as an entire village.

D This disaster could mirror the delicate conditions in which an ice sculpture can exist. It takes not only frigid temperatures and large quantities of frozen water, but determination and – for large structures – the financial prowess to recreate it repeatedly.

E And every year, to create these structures that visitors pay hundreds of euros a night to stay in, hundreds of thousands of tons of ice are carved and positioned. The blocks are fused together with 'snice' – a portmanteau of the words 'snow' and 'ice' – which has the consistency of soft, malleable ice that freezes after it is placed.

F In fact, in neighbouring China, some of the most impressive ice structures can be viewed annually in the city of Harbin. Located on the edge of Siberia, Harbin hosts a large ice and snow festival that features an entire village's worth of structures. Exquisitely detailed, these buildings and monuments provide an extravagant spectacle for millions of visitors each year.

G That, however, cannot be said about ice sculptures. Lasting as long as months or as little as minutes, one is never unaware of the transient nature of an ice sculpture. Why would someone spend hours carving what won't last much longer than it took to create?

H Designed by Russian architect Pyotr Yeropkin, its mammoth dimensions put it at around 20 metres tall and 50 metres wide. Interior features consisted of an ice 'garden', in which trees with ice birds perched on the branches filled the grounds. Although decorative, ice mattresses and ice pillows adorned rooms, and the outer walls were lined with delicate ice sculptures.

Vocabulary

A Complete the words in the sentences.

1 Many people draw i_ _ _ _ _ _ _ _ _ _ from older members of their family who struggled, but ultimately succeeded in making something of their lives.

2 Rather than having to be told what to do, Josie takes i_ _ _ _ _ _ _ _ _ at work and does what needs to be done.

3 Paul was let go due to his i_ _ _ _ _ _ _ _ _ at keeping company secrets, which led to the exposure of highly sensitive information.

4 Don't take my comments the wrong way; I really just meant to give you constructive c_ _ _ _ _ _ _ _.

5 Her loss at Wimbledon was really just a minor s_ _ _ _ _ _ ; the following year, she became a champion.

6 Due to the p_ _ _ _ _ _ _ _ _ of crime in the area, Don decided to look for a house elsewhere.

B Complete the sentences with these words.

> fast   high   mean   rosy   rough   rude

1 After graduating with first-class honours from university, Mike's family had _____ hopes that he'd make something out of his life.

2 If you think you can sail through life without working hard, you're in for a _____ awakening.

3 Just because Frank comes from the _____ streets of Boston it doesn't mean he's an unpleasant man.

4 She had a particularly _____ view of the situation, but everyone else was not so optimistic.

5 I'm not looking to invest years in this endeavour; I want a _____ track to success.

6 George has a very _____ manner, but he's quite sweet and gentle deep down.

C Circle the correct words.

1 Henry, these people are into a lot of dangerous stuff; you really don't want to fall down / in / up with them.

2 When Carol mentioned that Tom didn't get the promotion, she realised she had slipped in / up / out, as he didn't know about it.

3 They ended up being taken to the police station because they got caught / wound / taken up in an anti-government demonstration and some people there were acting aggressively.

4 When the publisher asked her if she wanted to be stationed in Japan, Donna skipped / leapt / flew at the chance.

5 Of / In / On all likelihood, they'll choose you to lead the team of scientists.

6 Things may be dull now, but good times are around the square / corner / block.

7 I know it's been a tough few weeks around here, but in perspective / retrograde / retrospect, we've learnt a lot about how our industry works.

8 He was a horrible boss to work for, but in / on / to his credit, he got things done.

D Complete the sentences with one word in each gap.

1 Don't _____ in the towel and quit your post just yet; give it another week.

2 Jason's dad had had it with him; he told him to _____ his act together and start looking for a job.

3 Many residents _____ out hope that more survivors would be found under the rubble.

4 Although she gave it her all in the final, she _____ short of getting a perfect mark by one point.

5 Despite only having done local theatre, Eric decided to _____ a real go of his acting career and he moved to New York.

6 After weeks of feeling nervous, Henry finally _____ up the courage to complain about how he was being treated in the company.

7 If singing is what you want to do in life, go for it; I won't try to _____ you back.

8 Don't just make plans for what you're going to do this year; think _____ and plan for the next five.

E Read the *Exam Reminder* and complete the *Exam Task*.

Exam Reminder

Dealing with words that have similar meanings

- Some of the four answer choices for vocabulary questions will have very similar meanings. They may be part of a set expression or, as is sometimes the case, the meaning is within the whole sentence.

- Look to see if the gap forms a set expression first and, if not, read the entire sentence closely to see what word choice will fit logically with the overall meaning.

Exam Task

For questions **1 – 8**, read the text below and decide which answer (**a**, **b**, **c** or **d**) best fits each gap.

A true Olympic triumph

Yusra Mardini is an Olympian like no other. A champion swimmer native to Damascus, she felt she had the **(1)** _____ of futures after war broke out in her home country of Syria. It essentially meant her plans for one day competing in the Olympic Games had been all but **(2)** _____ off. Fearing for her safety, she felt she had no choice but to **(3)** _____ out for the relative safety of Europe. She made her way across Turkey, eventually arriving at the shores of the Aegean and, like so many refugees, she undertook with dogged **(4)** _____ the journey over the perilous waters that lie between Turkey and the Greek island of Lesbos. Her boat, meant for six but carrying 20, couldn't make it the whole way; knowing their lives were **(5)** _____ stake, Mardini and two other strong swimmers got into the water and pushed the boat for three hours, eventually reaching land.

Some months later she would arrive in Germany, where she was able to pick up the **(6)** _____ of her life and get back on track. After training morning and evening for hours every day, she, along with ten other refugees, competed in the 2016 Rio Olympics. In the end, the **(7)** _____ she suffered during her flight from war did little to **(8)** _____ her spirits, and she remembers well that it was her swimming that saved her life and the lives of others.

1	a roughest	b	bleakest	c	crudest	d	harshest
2	a erased	b	written	c	deleted	d	marked
3	a sit	b	set	c	go	d	get
4	a prevalence	b	aptitude	c	fulfilment	d	determination
5	a to	b	on	c	in	d	at
6	a pieces	b	bits	c	fragments	d	parts
7	a ineptness	b	anguish	c	criticism	d	failure
8	a dampen	b	moisten	c	wet	d	drench

Grammar

Conditionals with & without *if*, inverted conditionals

A Rewrite the sentences using the word given. More than one answer may be possible.

1 If we don't learn how to solve problems, life will be difficult.
unless

_____

2 If we didn't give them shelter, they wouldn't survive the night.
providing

_____

3 If she had a choice, she would have studied abroad.
given

_____

4 You would have lost your house if you hadn't kept your job.
but

_____

5 Could John be president if the scandal hadn't occurred?
supposing

_____

6 You won't graduate from university if you don't pass your exams.
long

_____

B Complete the sentences with one word in each gap.

1 _____ she not failed to enter the academy, she could have been an astronaut.
2 _____ you to pull off this miraculous performance, you would astound the audience.
3 _____ for the last-minute reprieve, the prisoner would be dead.
4 _____ the state of finances at the firm, it's a wonder it didn't fail sooner.
5 _____ if you had won the lottery? Would you still be living in this flat?
6 _____ you had supplied the proper documents, they would have obtained passports.

Conditionals with continuous tenses; Mixed conditionals; *If* + modals, *going to*

C Complete the sentences with the correct form of the verbs in brackets. Use *would* if necessary.

1 If he'd taken bribes, he _____ (**not give**) a speech on corruption today.
2 Be prepared to put down a hefty deposit if you _____ (**search**) for a home.
3 Lightning would've struck you if you _____ (**stand**) outside in the storm.
4 If John weren't so habitually lazy, they _____ (**not fire**) him.
5 We could ask Molly about this if she _____ (**sit**) in front of us.
6 If the teacher had left the room, the whole class _____ (**cheat**) throughout the entire exam.
7 If you hadn't wrecked the car, we _____ (**drive**) to York now.
8 If you _____ (**go**) over to Kyle's house on Saturdays, he'd be playing computer games.

D Circle the correct words.

1 If you could / may complete this form, I'll be able to start the application process.
2 If we weren't / aren't going to move house together, then I'm moving without you!
3 If we must / might have dinner at the Jenson's, let's at least enjoy it when we're there.
4 If you would / will forget to feed their pet, they're bound to be very annoyed.
5 If I might / would like offer some advice, I think you should consider getting two jobs.
6 If they don't / won't come to the event, why am I sending them an invitation?

E Read the *Exam Reminder* and complete the *Exam Task*.

Exam Task

Read the passage, then select the word or phrase that fills the blank in both grammar and meaning.

The wisdom of teaching philosophy

The idea that children should be taught philosophy, (**1**) _____ it doesn't replace other pertinent subjects, has begun to pick up speed. Studies have shown that (**2**) _____ only does it enhance decision-making abilities, it (**3**) _____ also encourage children to look at things differently and approach problems from different angles. In a study I recently conducted, my team discovered that even the children recognise an improvement. One ten-year-old boy told me that if he (**4**) _____ studied philosophy at a younger age, he would (**5**) _____ a better problem solver today.

I wondered if anyone in the grown-up world would agree, so I began interviewing adults to see if my theory of philosophy being an effective decision-making tool (**6**) _____ be proved true. Michaela, a successful businesswoman with a master's degree in business, agreed to speak with me on (**7**) _____ that I did not reveal her full name. She freely admits that, after having struggled through many tough negotiating sessions throughout her career, she's now openly wondering, '(**8**) _____ if I had taken a degree in philosophy? I probably would have had easier success!'

1	a	supposing	b	as long as	c	unless	d	given
2	a	if	b	in	c	not	d	for
3	a	could	b	should	c	can	d	does
4	a	had	b	–	c	has	d	were
5	a	not have been	b	not be	c	have been	d	be
6	a	could	b	can	c	will	d	would
7	a	providing	b	condition	c	supposing	d	given
8	a	What	b	And	c	Only	d	As

Listening

A Read the *Exam Reminder*. What phrases in the *Exam Task* questions might be phrased differently in the recording?

_____

B [5.1] ▶️ Listen and complete the *Exam Task*.

Exam Task

You will hear a journalist talking about things that inspire both her and others. For questions **1–8**, complete the sentences with a word or short phrase.

1 The journalist is particularly impressed with the _____ of the musician she speaks about in the beginning.

2 Her reply to the musician is that _____ inspired her to be a journalist.

3 The interview with a _____ was one of the first the journalist conducted after qualifying.

4 The designer used _____ as inspiration for a women's wear collection.

5 Jessica states that observing _____ made her want to take up ballet.

6 While going to work, the architect would create _____ that would inspire him.

7 The architect used his _____ to create his most recent museum.

8 Tommy said that _____ is the top influence for the words of his songs.

C [5.2] ▶️ Listen again and check your answers.

writing: an essay (2)

Learning Reminder

Analysing contrasting texts

- When comparing two texts, decide if the texts are complimentary or contrasting. For the former, both texts will include shared views, whether positive or negative, and for the latter, there will be opposite ideas.

- Your essay must provide a summary, evaluation and reaction to two key points in each text. Find those key points and remember to summarise them in your own words, rather than copying them from the text

- Use advanced grammar to achieve a formal style in your essay.

A Read these three paragraphs. Which ones complement each other and which ones contrast?

1 Test anxiety is one of the biggest contributors to poor test marks. For some schoolchildren, no matter how much they study for an exam, they will panic during it and be unable to recall what they have learnt. It is imperative that schools move away from testing and use a more holistic approach to evaluation, such as in-class assessment by teachers.

2 As testing is a useful way to evaluate a person's knowledge, it's likely here to stay. That said, some students suffer with such anxiety that they can actually get sick in the middle of an exam. Teachers must ensure that every student gets a satisfactory amount of test preparation in class before national exams.

3 Administering aptitude tests to potential employees during the hiring process allows a company to maximise its business potential. While an interview provides assessment through human interaction, an aptitude test measures a candidate's abilities on a variety of skills, such as leadership, abstract reasoning and numerical aptitude. It is also an attractive option for testing skills due to the low administration costs.

B Which two paragraphs in exercise A do each of these partial essays relate to?

1 Tests are a fact of life that we must do our best to get used to. A person will be faced with testing at multiple stages in their life: as a young child, as an adolescent entering university and, in some cases, as a potential employee in a company. ☐ ☐

2 For some, no amount of test preparation is ever going to dissipate their nerves. For that reason, we must reconsider the testing process from the ground up and perhaps employ different methods of assessment. Given the current state of affairs, however, it would be unwise to ignore test preparation altogether. ☐ ☐

3 Employer aptitude testing is not likely to catch any potential candidate by surprise. The fact is that many university graduates will have sat numerous exams, such as school exams, national qualifications and the like, so a simple aptitude test is not likely to rattle their nerves. ☐ ☐

4 Testing might be viewed as an effective way of assessing one's skills. But in fact, very few other methods have really been tried out, at least not across the board. We shouldn't give up on developing better assessment tools, but on the bright side, a test gives a person a challenge to overcome. ☐ ☐

C Decide if the sentences are a summary (S), an evaluation (E) or a reaction (R).

1 All things considered, testing does provide insight into a person's abilities, but it can't reveal the whole picture. ☐
2 These tests cannot take the place of a face-to-face interview entirely. ☐
3 I'm convinced that if only computers were used to assess ability, our world would be a depressing place to live. ☐
4 On balance, I believe that when a person knows they are going to be tested, they should prepare thoroughly. ☐
5 Aptitude tests do not always give the most accurate reading of a person's abilities. ☐

D Read and complete the *Exam Task* below. Don't forget to use the *Useful Expressions* on page 77 of your Student's Book.

Exam Task

Read the two texts below. Write an **essay** summarising and evaluating the key points from both texts. Use your own words throughout as far as possible, and include your own ideas in your answers.

Write your answer in 240–280 words.

Standardised hiring tests

Giving aptitude tests to potential employees allows a company to maximise its potential. While an interview provides assessment through human interaction, an aptitude test measures abilities in a wide range of skills, such as leadership skills. It is also an attractive option for testing skills due to its low administration cost.

A case against testing

While tests can tell us many things about a person's intelligence, it is not always 100% reliable. Other factors, such as test anxiety, can affect the outcome. Cultural bias can also be an issue. A highly-skilled individual from India, for example, might perform poorly due to a language barrier, when they would be otherwise perfect for the job.

▶ Writing Reference p. 205 in Student's Book

Reading

A Read the *Exam Reminder*. What unfamiliar words do you see in the *Exam Task* article? Make a note of them and try to guess their meaning by using the text, if possible.

_____

B Now complete the *Exam Task*.

The art of the deal

Jack was the golden boy at his investment firm – young, handsome, optimistic, friendly, intelligent and hard-working. Jack arrived at work every morning with hope in his heart and the brass ring in his sights. His strength – and his only flaw – was that there was nothing that could stand in the way of him getting that ring – not failure, not fear – and as all were soon to see, despite his honest upbringing in a working-class family, not morality or even the law.

Such is what high-stakes investment banking can do to a man: corrupt the incorruptible, shade those born in the light, make the unbendable crooked. Having slaved away on the phones for months, nibbling on scraps instead of the seven-course meal that he wished for, Jack finally had a stroke of luck; he was assigned to retain one of the most powerful brokers in Chicago, Dwayne Hills, as a client of the firm. Known as the 'Axeman', Dwayne made his money by taking advantage, however legal the means, of every vulnerable company he set his sights on, which often resulted in many unfortunate employees getting the 'axe' from their jobs. Mercy was not a word in his vocabulary; nonetheless, he was every bit as respected as he was reviled and feared because, in short, he was a winner.

With an office decked out in extravagant Italian marble and a view of Lake Michigan, and the most exclusive real estate in downtown Chicago, Dwayne was not accustomed to meeting with small fish. For someone who makes millions of dollars a week, or even in a single transaction, it would take a miracle for someone from Jack's world to get a sit-down. But as impatient as Jack was to snag a high roller as his investor, he bided his time and used his gifted imagination to cook up a plan, just waiting for the right moment. Knowing Dwayne's penchant for fine art, Jack decided to give Dwayne an original Joan Miró sculpture that his late uncle had willed to him – an object whose value was equal to a year of Jack's salary.

Small but extremely well-crafted and remarkable to behold, Jack had it encased in an oak box with a viewing window. He knew that such a powerful, influential and infamous power broker would never enter through the main entrance, so at the crack of dawn on the 23rd of September, with the box in both hands, he waited hopefully around the back of Dwayne's office building for him to arrive. A sleek black town car pulled into the alley and stopped. The driver exited the vehicle and proceeded to open the passenger door. Dwayne stepped out, with his polished black patent-leather shoes, tailored suit and slicked-back light brown hair. He looked head to toe like a man made of money.

Jack's eyes lit up. Instinctively, he stepped forward without hesitating for a second and, beaming, said 'Happy Birthday, Mr Hills'. The corners of Dwayne's mouth turned up slightly and his eyes softened, for he saw what was inside the small wooden box with the delicate red bow, and he instantly knew the consideration that had gone into the gift, the selection of the meeting place and the timing – even though it wasn't his birthday – and he couldn't help but feel enamoured of this impetuous whippersnapper. Dwayne stood in front of Jack, paused with a growing grin and said, 'You've got two minutes to tell me something that I don't already know and is going to make me a million bucks by sundown.'

Jack knew this was his one and only moment to impress Dwayne. He rattled off a bunch of half-baked ideas that Dwayne shot down like clay pigeons at a shooting range. Dwayne's phone rang with Jack in mid-sentence and Jack knew his chance was slipping away, so he had to think big, and fast. He knew his mother's publicly-traded company was facing a very damaging inspection review, which was to be published in a week's time. As soon as Dwayne's call ended, Jack pressured him to invest in Diamond Autos – a suggestion which Dwayne scoffed at. 'This is it, kid? Is this all you've got for me?' Jack, knowing that he had just breached laws against insider trading, gave Dwayne a sharp, almost devious look that, in his decades of business dealings, was immediately recognised as suggesting a sure-fire thing whose origins are best left unknown.

You are going to read an extract from a novel about corporate greed. For questions **1 – 6**, choose the answer (**a**, **b**, **c** or **d**) which you think fits best according to the text.

1 What aspect of Jack's identity revealed in the first paragraph seems to contradict his readiness to break the law?

   a how he was raised

   b his viewpoint on life

   c how he treats others

   d his determination to succeed

2 What kind of reputation does Dwayne Hills have?

   a He is simply despised and feared by all.

   b He is viewed as a corrupt and ruthless man.

   c He is known for turning ailing businesses around.

   d He is held in very high regard by his peers.

3 How does the author characterise Jack's efforts to meet with Dwayne?

   a as an uncalculated stab in the dark

   b as an exercise in self-sacrifice

   c as a lucky roll of the dice

   d as an exercise in trial and error

4 Considering how and where Jack waited for Dwayne, we can infer that

   a someone tipped Jack off about Dwayne's habits.

   b Jack must have seen Dwayne's vehicle pull up around the back.

   c most people know where Dwayne usually enters his building.

   d Jack is well-aware of powerful men's routines.

5 What did Dwayne feel about Jack upon meeting him?

   a His ambush was inappropriate and pitiful.

   b His look was that of a well-informed man.

   c His worth needed to be proved.

   d His ingenuity had him sold.

6 At what point did Jack abandon his morals?

   a the moment he saw Dwayne

   b during Dwayne's call

   c upon hearing Dwayne's reaction

   d while he was pitching ideas

Vocabulary

A Complete the words in the sentences.

1 Although somewhat beneficial, the economic **s**_____ wasn't enough to jumpstart the economy completely.

2 Lisa's demand for hush money was reported to the police as a case of **b**_____.

3 Bill urged Robbie not to **s**_____ a golden opportunity to invest in a winning venture.

4 She's not the owner of the company – she's just a **p**_____ who was sent to represent the company.

5 The lawyers presented David with a generous **s**_____ that he accepted rather than go to court.

6 Ronald was suspended from his post during the internal investigation into his **m**_____ of company funds.

7 While the company implied at the beginning that they would not move on the price, in the end they made **c**_____ and accepted the lower offer.

8 If we discontinue our best-selling product, the company will **i**_____ such losses that it will have to shut.

B Circle the correct words.

1 Helen, don't be such a stingy / miserly / spendthrift – you'll be broke by the end of the month.

2 If you keep up these shady / lavish / moneyed dealings, you'll have to answer to the police.

3 Everything he did seemed well-to-do / above board / penny-pinching, so it was a shock when the commissioner placed him under investigation.

4 The boss's son had a(n) well-kept / entitled / wanting air about him that no one liked.

5 I'm afraid I've got to ask for an advance on my pay cheque; I'm in a bit of a tight angle / corner / bend.

6 Being a supervisor and giving jobs to unqualified friends is a(n) extravagant / corrupt / thrifty way of employing people.

7 My parents provided well for my brother and me; we didn't have to go / be / have without even once.

8 I think people are taking a little money out of the till, so we're going to have to smash / crack / smack down on this before it gets out of control.

C Complete the sentences with these words.

abuse bet bribery cuts opulent red soar tape

1 When the cost of fuel began to _____, Karla started taking the bus more often.

2 The president arranged for his nephew to be released without being charged – a clear _____ of his powers.

3 If we continue operating in the _____ for much longer, we'll have to close down.

4 The patient was charged with _____ for asking a hospital worker to give him special treatment in exchange for money.

5 Wow, this _____ chandelier must have set you back a fortune!

6 Putting your money in savings to accrue a little interest is often the safest _____ for an investment.

7 Due to _____ they've made to the budget, everybody must watch their business expenses more closely.

8 There's so much red _____ to wade through when applying for a government grant, but that's how bureaucracy works.

D Complete the sentences with one word in each gap.

1 The bottom _____ is that you need to rein in your spending before you're flat broke.

2 The man reported the driver to the police when he tried to rob him _____ his wallet.

3 She works full-time during the week, but makes extra money on the _____ waitressing at the weekend.

4 Because of the crash, Martin had to spend most of his nest _____.

5 Kyle knew someone had tipped the police _____ when he got arrested for illegal gambling.

6 A few Wall Street brokers live life in the fast _____, but it never lasts very long.

7 Gina's uncle willed his entire fortune to her, so when he passed on, she came _____ a lot of money.

8 As a _____ resort, Mary and Tom went to Tom's parents for an emergency loan.

E Read the *Exam Reminder* and complete the *Exam Task*.

Exam Reminder

Exam Task

For questions **1 – 8**, read the text below and decide which answer (**a**, **b**, **c** or **d**) best fits each gap.

A price on happiness?

The phrase 'Money doesn't buy happiness' is a cautionary cliché that keeps us from blindly lining our pockets with (**1**) _____ in the hope that we'll feel happier. But a recent study at Princeton University in New Jersey is challenging that idea; the study suggests that happiness could possibly be (**2**) _____ at an annual income of the equivalent of approximately $75,000 US dollars. Can that be true?

Dealing with multiple-choice cloze texts
- Skim over the text for the main idea and then look closely at the gaps. Decide what part of speech goes in each gap by looking at the words surrounding the gap.
- Remember that the normal rules do not always apply to fixed phrases and idioms, so you will need to check your answer carefully and make sure it sounds right.

Hearing this, we might be tempted to run to our employer and pressure them to (**3**) _____ out the cash more generously because our happiness depends on it. Of course, they're not likely to (**4**) _____ us with money just so that we smile more often in our cubicles. So before we start thinking a little extra dough is going to (**5**) _____ us for our sadness, it's important to note that the study makes a distinction between types of happiness – daily happiness and lifelong satisfaction.

For the former, no amount of money makes a difference, whether you're frequently (**6**) _____ or you're rolling in it. For the latter, though, the study showed that people making less than the magic number seem to express more frustration about the problems in their lives, for example, a health issue, whereas more (**7**) _____ folks aren't as affected by the same problem. Interestingly, though, those past the marker expressed no more satisfaction with life than those that just reached it. This suggests that a(n) (**8**) _____ to a multi-billion-dollar fortune wouldn't be any more satisfied than someone making a paltry $75,000 a year. What a waste!

1	a	stash	b	hoard	c	stock	d	dosh
2	a	cherished	b	prized	c	treasured	d	valued
3	a	crack	b	dole	c	tip	d	toss
4	a	rinse	b	wash	c	shower	d	bathe
5	a	reimburse	b	balance	c	offset	d	compensate
6	a	skint	b	thrifty	c	posh	d	shady
7	a	well-heeled	b	big-hearted	c	open-handed	d	tight-fisted
8	a	proxy	b	heir	c	chancellor	d	treasurer

Grammar

Inversion; *So & such*; Unreal Past; *Would rather, would prefer & had better*

A Each sentence has one incorrect word. Cross it out and write the correct word. More than one answer may be possible.

1 Hardly was she completed the form when she was denied the loan.   _____
2 Under no situations should you send cash through the post.   _____
3 Only if there was a co-signer did they approve the mortgage.   _____
4 Not after he entered university did he have to pay his own bills.   _____
5 On no credit should anyone sink millions of pounds into an indebted company.   _____
6 Seldom will Helen monitored her teenage son's spending habits.   _____
7 At a point did he ever say no to a credit card offer.   _____
8 Never had Bill felt so much stress than when he loses all his money on that scheme.   _____

B Complete the sentences with *so* or *such*.

1 He was surprised when they denied him the loan because he had _____ good credit.
2 _____ was her standing in the community that they threw her a party for her birthday.
3 _____ inept was Michael at maths that it was a wonder how he became an accountant.
4 _____ complicated was that transaction that it took six employees to sort it out.
5 Neil had _____ much money in the bank, he had to open another account.
6 The work that went into the business transfer was _____ a waste of time – it didn't even go through!

C Complete the sentences with these phrases.

| as if   better   had better   if only   it's time   wish   would prefer   would rather |

1 I'm freezing, so I _____ to sit inside instead of out in the open air.
2 You _____ take care of these payments before they're considered late.
3 I think _____ we talked about Paul's runaway finances.
4 _____ Dad would loan me this money, I could start my own business.
5 I think I _____ take on a bit of debt and get educated than have no education at all.
6 They _____ they could afford to get married in a castle.
7 Melanie behaves _____ she's the heiress to a great empire, rather than her dad's two shops.
8 George had _____ speak to a therapist about his gambling addiction.

D Complete the text with one word in each gap.

Advice that makes 'cents'

Before going off to university, my dad, an accountant, sat me down and said, 'It's time we (**1**) _____ a good long talk about money.' He had some sound advice for me really; if (**2**) _____ everyone were so lucky to get (**3**) _____ advice! He told me that (**4**) _____ no circumstances should I ever get a credit card. Of course, (**5**) _____ did he know I already had one, but I understood that he meant for me to be careful with it and not (**6**) _____ I really needed to did I use it. He also told me that on (**7**) _____ account should I lend someone more money than I was willing to part with forever. That piece of advice really stuck with me and not (**8**) _____ have I ever forgotten it.

E Read the *Exam Reminder* and complete the *Exam Task*.

Exam Task

For questions **1 – 5**, complete the second sentence so that it has a similar meaning to the first sentence, using the word given. **Do not change the word given.** You must use between **three** and **eight** words, including the word given.

1 Always using cash was Lisa's preference for payment.

   prefer

   Lisa _____ always use cash to pay for things.

2 The profits were so terrible that the business closed after one month.

   such

   The business closed after a month because _____ profits.

3 Jonathan couldn't explain his debt at all.

   reason

   Concerning his debt, _____ Jonathan give for it.

4 Catherine waited until she had finished eating to discuss finances.

   only

   As regards finances, _____ discuss them.

5 They went shopping as soon as they got their lottery winnings.

   sooner

   _____ than they went shopping.

Exam Reminder

Recognising structures

- Key word transformation exercises require you to recognise structures, both in the sentence you're given and the part of the sentence you need to complete. Look for sentences that require inversion or verb tense changes.
- Remember to check that your rewritten sentence contains all of the details from the first sentence.

Listening

A Read the *Exam Reminder*. What themes and attitudes are present in the *Exam Task*?

_____

B 6.1 ▶️ Listen and complete the *Exam Task*.

Exam Reminder

Considering themes & attitudes

- Before you listen, remember to read the questions to identify the unifying theme across the two tasks.
- Look more carefully at each task to identify what aspect of that theme it covers.
- Think about what you know about the theme and then try to predict what attitudes may be expressed by the speakers in each task.

Exam Task

You will hear five short extracts in which different people talk about how they handle debt.

Task 1

For questions **1 – 5**, choose from the list (**A – H**) how each speaker got into debt.

While you listen, you must complete both tasks.

A a matter of life or death
B letting friends use your card
C extravagant lifestyle
D negligent behaviour
E something that crept up slowly
F fraudulent use
G peer pressure
H poor role models

1	Speaker 1	☐	4	Speaker 4	☐
2	Speaker 2	☐	5	Speaker 5	☐
3	Speaker 3	☐			

Task 2

For questions **6 – 10**, choose from the list (**A – H**) how each speaker feels about debt.

A uncontrollable matter
B nagging reminder
C debilitating burden
D something we live with
E overblown worry
F the bank's responsibility
G unfair circumstance
H a matter for the courts

6	Speaker 1	☐	9	Speaker 4	☐
7	Speaker 2	☐	10	Speaker 5	☐
8	Speaker 3	☐			

C 6.2 ▶️ Listen again and check your answers.

Writing: an essay (3)

Learning Reminder

Choosing between two topics

- When choosing between two topics, read both prompts and consider what you are being asked to do in each, whether it be presenting an argument or discussing the pros and cons of an issue.
- For each topic, underline key words, outline the major points to discuss and think about the vocabulary you will have to use. Once you've got a good idea of what each prompt is asking of you, choose the one you're most comfortable with.

A Read the prompts and decide if they are asking you to consider one specific question (A), to discuss two sides of an issue (B) or to choose between two opinions and discuss (C).

1 Should children receive money to do household chores or should they be taught that this is an unpaid responsibility? ☐

2 If a company goes bankrupt, should executives be forced to compensate employees, even if it bankrupts them? ☐

3 How is giving a bribe a disadvantage to you and how it is a disadvantage to society at large? ☐

4 Should people buy locally, even if it's more expensive, or should they get the best bargains they can find, no matter the origin? ☐

5 How are people who reveal corruption a benefit to society and how are they a traitor to their employer? ☐

B Read these two prompts and label them A, B or C as you did for the prompts in exercise A. Underline the key words as they pertain to the task at hand. Then match the phrases to the prompts you would use them for. You will not use all the phrases.

Prompt 1 _____

Microloans are very small loans given by banks in third-world countries to help families start small businesses. Proponents say it gives prospective merchants a helping hand. Critics say it drives families into debt. In what ways can loans be beneficial for borrowers?

_____

_____

Prompt 2 _____

Crimes such as corruption, fraud, insider trading and identity theft are non-violent crimes and, as such, are labelled 'white-collar crimes'. These criminals go to different, sometimes nicer, prisons than violent offenders. Is it important to keep white-collar criminals separate or should they live with other criminals?

_____

_____

> community service   dreams fulfilled   early release   helping the poor   high interest rates
> jumpstart the economy   predatory lending   punishment fits the crime   rehabilitation programme
> safety concerns   severity of offence   stepping stone

C Read the sentences and decide which prompt (1 or 2) in the *Exam Task* they belong to.

1 It is easy to use them to pay for things, rather than carrying around a lot of cash. ☐

2 Let's consider a car manufacturer that has been hiding the fact that its cars have been failing safety tests. ☐

3 Their careers suffer because other companies may be wary of hiring them. ☐

4 Not saying anything makes them guilty, but betraying their employer could end their career. ☐

5 They can build up a debt quickly, and then be stuck with a bill they cannot pay. ☐

6 The higher the balance, the more money that is paid in interest, which can be quite high. ☐

D Read and complete the *Exam Task* below. Don't forget to use the *Useful Expressions* on page 91 of your Student's Book.

Exam Task

Choose from one of the two topics to write your **essay** about. You have 30 minutes and should write up to two pages.

Prompt 1

A whistle-blower is an employee who, having discovered wrongdoing in a company, exposes this information to the public, breaking confidentiality agreements and often risking their safety. How do they benefit society and why are they considered traitors? Discuss and give specific examples to support your views.

Prompt 2

With credit cards being so prevalent, it's quite likely that once adolescents leave home, they'll start using them and perhaps risk their financial well-being due to misuse. Should parents recommend their university-aged children get credit cards or should they instil in them a policy of credit card abstinence? Support your opinion with reasons and examples.

▶ Writing Reference p. 205 in Student's Book

Review 3   Units 5 & 6

Vocabulary

A **Choose the correct answers.**

1 The plaintiff rejected the measly _____ and decided to go to court.

  a reimbursement   **b** concession

  c settlement   **d** compensation

2 The whole class was _____ awe of Michael's oil painting of his dog, Silo.

  a for   **b** with

  c on   **d** in

3 His talent meant he could create wondrous things, but his _____ meant he hardly ever felt like working.

  a adversity   **b** lethargy

  c ineptitude   **d** failure

4 In many developing nations, there is a _____ of corruption in their governments which threatens positive growth.

  a aspiration   **b** fulfilment

  c prevalence   **d** perseverance

5 Every time I'm seen with a _____ politician, it damages my reputation.

  a broken   **b** wanting

  c crooked   **d** moneyed

6 The film shoot suffered a _____ when a hurricane destroyed half the sets.

  a payback   **b** backhander

  c backbone   **d** setback

7 Fresh funds provided the _____ for the company to get back on its feet.

  a blackmail   **b** margin

  c bribery   **d** stimulus

8 You can _____ off going to university if you fail all your final exams.

  a write   **b** pay

  c check   **d** tick

9 The greedy man wouldn't hesitate to _____ away his valued assets if he thought it would bring him more money.

  a wager   **b** bet

  c gamble   **d** stake

10 After the racing accident, everyone wished the driver a _____ recovery.

  a snappy   **b** hasty

  c rosy   **d** speedy

11 If I were you, I wouldn't _____ your chances at making this investment work.

  a thump   **b** bash

  c crack   **d** blow

12 With the amount of money the candidate has spent on the election, he _____ the best chance of winning.

  a stands   **b** walks

  c leaps   **d** jumps

13 Margie _____ at the chance to work on a tropical island.

  a leapt   **b** slipped

  c hopped   **d** sprang

14 After the devastating loss at the championship, the athlete took some time to _____ up the pieces and get back into training.

  a grab   **b** select

  c choose   **d** pick

15 Having failed two classes, Greg decided to turn over a new _____ and start studying harder.

  a page   **b** leaf

  c sheet   **d** plate

16 If you _____ this brilliant opportunity to make a go of your life, I'll never forgive you.

  a squabble   **b** squash

  c squander   **d** squat

17 While her boss was away, Janice took the _____ and got things done without instruction.

  a propensity   **b** initiative

  c determination **d** foresight

18 Be careful when taking an unlicensed taxi; the driver might just _____ you off.

  a split   **b** tear

  c rip   **d** shred

19 Mark vowed to stop being lazy and take more exercise, but his friends knew better – a _____ doesn't change its spots.

  a leopard   **b** cheetah

  c jaguar   **d** panther

20 As much as the candidate tried to convince people of his honesty, he couldn't shake off his _____ past.

  a serene   **b** tranquil

  c shady   **d** frigid

Grammar

B Choose the correct answers.

1 Had it not been for Michael's strong recommendation, James _____ been hired.

  a would have   **b** wouldn't have

  c hadn't   **d** hasn't

2 _____ we fix this hole in the budget, we'll be bankrupt in six months.

  a Supposing   **b** Unless

  c Providing   **d** Provided

3 Not _____ did Josephine ask for anyone to chip in for the camping supplies.

  a sooner   **b** only

  c after   **d** once

4 But for her doctor's note, Jane _____ the opportunity to retake her exam.

  a would have lost   **b** would lose

  c wouldn't have lost **d** wouldn't lose

5 He left university with not too much debt, _____ the expensive tuition he had to pay.

  a so long as   **b** as long

  c on condition   **d** given

6 If they _____ notes in class, I would have noticed something.

  a were passing   **b** passed

  c had been passing **d** have been passing

7 Not _____ person could vouch for Jim's whereabouts on the night of the murder.

  a until   **b** only

  c one   **d** single

8 I know you don't want to face the music, but it's time you _____ yourself in to the authorities.

  a turn   **b** turned

  c will turn   **d** are turning

9 If you had practised your Italian, you'd _____ like a native already.

  a spoke   **b** be speaking

  c have spoken   **d** have been speaking

10 _____ was the determination of the researcher that the success of her project was only a matter of time.

  a So   **b** Little

  c Much   **d** Such

11 Barely _____ the building when his manager called him back in.

  a did Leon leave   **b** was Leon leaving

  c had Leon left   **d** was Leon to leave

12 If you _____ wear a suit to the party, wear a lively one with a bit of colour!

  a might   **b** will

  c must   **d** could

13 It was _____ tedious a chore that Nigella couldn't finish it in one go.

  a such   **b** so

  c such a   **d** so much

14 If she had obtained her master's degree, she could _____ the current supervisor of her department.

  a not have been   **b** had been

  c have been   **d** be

15 Only _____ you suddenly win the lottery will you be able to pay off that debt.

  a by   **b** whether

  c for   **d** if

16 If she hadn't got involved in a doping scandal, the crowd would _____ her performance at the moment.

  a not be cheering   **b** have cheered

  c cheer   **d** be cheering

17 If he hadn't entered the country illegally, he wouldn't _____ the police when he goes out.

  a have been avoiding **b** be avoiding

  c have avoided   **d** avoid

18 _____ Barry had given us advance notice about the event.

  a Only if   **b** It's time

  c If only   **d** If

19 If you _____ answer a few short questions first, I'll be happy to arrange a meeting with the loan officer.

  a wouldn't like to   **b** must

  c might   **d** would like to

20 We _____ to leave at six in the morning.

  a would prefer not   **b** would rather not

  c had better   **d** had better not

Use of English

C Read the text below and decide which answer (a, b, c or d) best fits each gap.

Savings plan

Saving up for a nest (1) _____ is an important part of life and should not be ignored, no matter how young or how (2) _____ you are. For the latter, it's not much of a worry; such are the lives of the (3) _____ few. But the rest of us, who, quite frankly, make up the majority of the population, have to (4) _____ at times. Besides, thinking (5) _____ about such things builds character and shows how responsible you can be, not to mention alleviates worries about growing old and being flat (6) _____.

So how much should you be saving annually? If you (7) _____ out to retire with, say, a quarter of a million pounds, you can do this by investing 2,000 pounds a year in a high-interest account, starting at the age of 25. But do you really need that much? In all (8) _____, you won't, so even half the amount will allow for a comfortable life.

1	**a**	stone	**b**	egg	**c**	seed	**d**	pit
2	**a**	well-kept	**b**	well-oiled	**c**	well-off	**d**	well-bred
3	**a**	privileged	**b**	wanting	**c**	entitled	**d**	opulent
4	**a**	stingy	**b**	spendthrift	**c**	greedy	**d**	penny pinch
5	**a**	ahead	**b**	above	**c**	over	**d**	beyond
6	**a**	needy	**b**	bust	**c**	poor	**d**	broke
7	**a**	get	**b**	set	**c**	let	**d**	bet
8	**a**	prospect	**b**	chance	**c**	opportunity	**d**	likelihood

D Complete the text with the correct form of the words in bold.

Beware of what inspires you

People get (1) _____ from a variety of sources. We're conditioned to believe that **INSPIRE**
it should be something moving, such as a beautiful landscape, a touching work of art,
or a well-crafted story. For many people, though, they derive their (2) _____ from **MOTIVATE**
how much money they'll make from a particular endeavour. Money does allow us to live
comfortable lives; for those who like to live (3) _____, they need a lot of it to do so, **EXTRAVAGANT**
and then there are some (4) _____ folks who simply like accumulating it but never **MISER**
spending it. Much (5) _____, though, is levied at people who sacrifice decency in **CRITICISE**
the pursuit of money. And so often, when looking at the corporate world and the
actions that take place in this environment, it's not hard to find stories of people
taking bribes or of officials involved in the (6) _____ of funds. There's also an **USE**
aggressiveness that persists in how people do business; like hawks, they wait to
snatch up a(n) (7) _____ property in the hope of turning a profit, even at the expense **VALUE**
of low-income residents who are (8) _____ to stop it. But as the saying goes, it is **POWER**
not the person who has too little, but the one who craves more, that is poor.

E Read the text below and think of the word which best fits each gap. Use only one word in each gap.

19 July
Decisions, decisions!

Summer's almost over and in a year I'll be leaving school. My mum has been nagging me to make a decision about what I want to do afterwards. If (1) _____ these decisions were easier! My first thought is to have a gap year, but (2) _____ I enjoy having all that free time to myself? What if I don't want to continue my education? Of course, my parents would (3) _____ I go to university straight away, but I haven't decided what I want to do, and (4) _____ if I make a hasty choice and follow the wrong course? I suppose if I (5) _____ gone to the career seminar last month, I (6) _____ have a better idea of what path to follow. I meant to go, but (7) _____ sooner had I enrolled than my best friend Marcy persuaded me to take a weekend trip to the Lake District with her parents. On the bright side, it's not too late to consider all my options and I'm not sure hurrying into a decision is (8) _____ a great idea. Mum will understand!

F Complete the second sentence so that it has a similar meaning to the first sentence, using the word given. Do not change the word given. You must use between three and eight words, including the word given.

1 They wouldn't have lost the match if the coach hadn't interfered.
but
As regards the match, _____ won it.

2 If the entrance fee is reasonable, I'll attend the conference.
providing
I'll _____ is reasonable.

3 The group are in agreement about Stacy moving out.
time
They all agree that _____ out.

4 It'll be too late to apply if you don't do it today.
better
You _____ late to do it.

5 Mark can be quite irritable and that's why he gets into arguments so often.
were
If Mark _____ into arguments so often.

6 Pablo said she was not to open the door for any reason.
under
Pablo said _____ the door.

Reading

A Read the *Exam Reminder*. How does the author begin the story in the first paragraph of the *Exam Task*?

_____

B Now complete the *Exam Task*.

Exam Reminder

Checking for cohesion
- Connections between paragraphs are not always immediately recognisable from the concluding sentences of one paragraph and introductory sentences of the next paragraph.
- Pay close attention to the sentences before and after the gap as a lot of the most important information will be there.
- In the event that linking and referencing phrases do not give away the answer, read the paragraphs carefully and look for situations, scenarios or experiences that are continued by one of the missing paragraphs.

Cave exploration has been a lifelong obsession for me. I was lucky enough to have grown up about half a kilometre from a cave as a child, as well as to have a cave enthusiast as a father. He and I travelled to that cave several times a year, weather permitting, and each and every time we visited, we found something new that kept us wanting to come back again and again. **1** ▢

On our next trip, we decided to gather together some tools: a small hammer, a chisel and a cordless hand-held drill, to see if we could chip enough of the sides away to squeeze through. It wouldn't take much; the material around the hole had worn away, probably from the elements. After about an hour, the space was big enough for me to fit through and I was all set to go, except my dad insisted he go first, for safety reasons, of course. **2** ▢

If I may just add here, this is the sort of moment that has compelled me to make potholing an integral part of my life. I've had many such moments like this in my exploratory quests, such as the moment I discovered a cavernous lake which, upon further inspection after my fellow potholer and I returned with diving equipment, led to another, previously-unexplored and water-accessible-only section. **3** ▢

I wouldn't classify myself as a professional or anything, but that kind of recognition makes you proud of what you do, even if it's more or less a hobby. But going back to that moment with my dad, it's a moment – probably the first such 'Wow' moment I had in my life, aside from unwrapping a birthday present – that I carry with me every single time I venture into a cave, be it one already explored or a new one in some far-off land. **4** ▢

We explored the new area for what seemed like an eternity, perhaps because I never wanted it to end. There is a mix of excitement and trepidation upon discovering a new area like this because, even though I knew cave monsters didn't exist, you always have this vague thought in the back of your mind that some strange Neolithic mammal with razor-sharp teeth and a voracious appetite is going to lunge at you. **5** ▢

On top of that, we were in a strange sort of crevasse, making it difficult to manoeuvre. I could sense that my fellow potholer was searching for the switch on his lamp and then I heard a noise that made me think, 'Oops, there goes a pick.' You're totally helpless at this point – no mobile signal, no way to even reach a mobile, no light, although I knew Mike would find his. You can't even yell for help because no one would hear you or something unpleasant would instead. **6** ▢

For this and many other reasons, potholing is like exploring a new universe just on the other side of our physical plane of existence. It's underneath the surface of the Earth and it contains wonders not found anywhere above ground, each of which is otherworldly and spectacular. And as I've said, you never know what you're going to find, and there is no shortage of gasps of amazement no matter how many times you explore one. **7** ▢

We've visited caves in North America quite frequently, where there is a lifetime of cave exploration to draw on, and through potholing connections we've managed to explore many which are off the beaten track. I'm truly lucky to have experienced this unique pleasure throughout my life. A quote from American writer Joseph Campbell often gets stuck in my head: 'The cave you fear to enter holds the treasure you seek.' I know he's speaking figuratively, but I'm quite happy to follow it in the literal sense as well.

You are going to read a story about cave exploration. Seven paragraphs have been removed from the story. Choose from the paragraphs **A – H** the one which fits each gap (**1 – 7**). There is one extra paragraph which you do not need to use.

A Or the time when that same colleague and I found prehistoric cave drawings in a section. We were featured in a potholing journal after that – we actually made the front cover: a photo of myself and my colleague, and behind us were etchings of horses and some kind of prehistoric bull that you'd never see on any farm any more.

B Again, I don't believe in mad cave dwellers, but at such moments, logic can escape you. You have to tell yourself to calm down, even laugh a little at your predicament. And just like that – 'click!' – Mike finds his light switch and all is back to normal – a 'Phew!' moment, of which all us potholers have had just as many as 'Wow!' and 'Whoa!' moments.

C For instance, once I stumbled upon a small opening that I hadn't seen before. It was no bigger than the width of my glove and there was no way I'd be able to fit through it. I told my dad to shine his torch at it and, to our shock, there was another section of the cavern on the other side. I could feel a gentle breeze and I would later learn the potholers' saying, 'If it blows, it goes': this was worth exploring.

D With just a few more taps of the hammer, it was finally wide enough for my dad to squeeze through. It was a rather thrilling moment and I felt we were like explorers of the new world, looking to see what treasures it had to offer. Once he was through, I passed the torch to Dad and I then heard a long 'Whoa!' that stirred up butterflies in my stomach.

E I still go potholing with my dad, even after all these years. Although we've more or less retired from our local cave – which, incidentally, has since been transformed into a tourist attraction due to our discoveries – we've crossed borders and explored some of the most impressive caves in the world.

F Other such fears are fed by the feeling that you can become trapped in a tight space or that you'll suffer from equipment failure and be left without vision. I remember a time once when I was potholing with my colleague and the torch on my helmet blew out. He hadn't turned on his helmet torch and we were far down enough that no light from the entrance could reach us. I couldn't even see my hand in front of my face.

G And of course, I sometimes feel like hanging up the helmet torch just for an easy life. There's nothing wrong with going on an organised tour every once in a while, one that includes a visit to a cavern snack bar or features a cable car that takes you back to the top. Besides, were it not for those tours, most people might not even step foot in a cave in their entire lives, which would make me a little sad.

H At that moment, I was naturally anxious to see what he was gazing at, so I crawled through myself. The cavern was probably three times as big as the one we had already explored before. The smells were fresh and indicative of plant life. I wondered in passing if we were about to discover a new species of fern or a rare type of moss.

Vocabulary

A **Complete the sentences with these words.**

> buzz   drain   eye   tip   track   whim

1 Not content with guided tours, Johann always went off the beaten _____.
2 They didn't plan to go to Lapland; they just got in a car and drove there on a _____.
3 The _____ around the camp is that the forest patrol is going to start fining people with expired permits.
4 The entrance to the cave was just the _____ of the iceberg; it reached depths of one kilometre.
5 The construction of the sprawling shopping centre has been a real _____ on public resources.
6 Few of the gaudy trinkets on sale in the bazaar caught Marion's _____.

B **Circle the correct words.**

1 The invasion / injection of enemy forces was the source of great misery for the inhabitants.
2 Something looks out of world / place here; I think we've been burgled.
3 The breakdown in basic services spelt / spoke disaster for the community.
4 Being twice swindled on holiday left a strong / bitter taste in Paul's mouth.
5 She claims to have sighted a supernatural oddity / phenomenon in the abandoned hotel.
6 One wrong move on the mountain could mean the variation / difference between life and death.
7 On the last day of their trip, they decided to satisfy / indulge themselves a little, so they visited a spa.
8 Garry used a torch to wipe / drive the bear out of his lair.

C Complete the sentences with the correct form of the words in bold.

1 As their caravan wound around the steep mountainside, a _____ village revealed itself in the distance. — **PICTURE**

2 If I had to make an _____ guess, I'd say you were a professor of anthropology. — **EDUCATE**

3 She found many things _____ about the region; the poverty, the pollution, the smell. — **DESIRE**

4 His _____ meant he could walk into an area full of ferocious wild animals and not be the least bit scared. — **FEAR**

5 The morbid tale was too much for Hank to bear, given how the storyteller told it so _____. — **GRAPH**

6 She couldn't go on holiday with Jonathan; they had too much emotional _____ . — **BAG**

7 Beth was an early riser; sleeping in was a _____ for her. — **RARE**

8 Having grown up in the countryside, Oscar still had a _____ way about himself even after living in the city for a few years. — **PROVINCE**

D Complete the text with one word in each gap.

25 Feb

While in Hawaii, my fellow travellers and I decided on the (**1**) _____ of the moment that we'd trek through a nearby rainforest. It was a well-travelled area, so we decided there'd be no need to plan and we'd play it by (**2**) _____. My friends Derrick and Joe stumbled (**3**) _____ a faint trail that they wanted to investigate. I warned them that it might be dangerous, as it wasn't well-marked, but it didn't dawn (**4**) _____ them that there could be a reason for that. Joe just replied, 'Oh come, Henry … where's your (**5**) _____ of adventure?' As they headed (**6**) _____, my partner Vicky and I ventured further into the forest on the well-marked trail, thinking that they'd (**7**) _____ up with us later. When that never happened, we panicked and called the forestry service. No sooner had we called the number than Joe and Derrick appeared. It turned out they were never more than a stone's (**8**) _____ from us the whole time.

E Read the *Exam Reminder* and complete the *Exam Task*.

Exam Reminder

Understanding new words

- The stems and roots of words can provide clues to meanings. They might be related to other languages you know and are often related to other words in English.
- Have a look at these stems and roots and think of other words that are similar. Remember to try all options in the sentence before choosing your answer.

Exam Task

Choose the word or phrase that best completes the sentence.

1 Sarah has a(n) _____ for knowledge; she's always reading.

   a thirst   c appetite
   b hunger   d craving

2 The Colossus of Rhodes was one of the seven ancient _____ of the world.

   a marvels   c spectacles
   b wonders   d rarities

3 Democracy allows for a(n) _____ of views to be expressed.

   a necessity   c intensity
   b adversity   d diversity

4 He gave a _____ response to his opponent that impressed the audience.

   a narrow-minded   c short-sighted
   b quick-witted   d long-winded

5 Margie was an _____ traveller; even dangerous conflict wouldn't stop her from visiting a place.

   a intrepid   c ingenious
   b inquisitive   d insightful

6 The entire population of great crested newts was _____ when they built the motorway.

   a wiped up   c wiped off
   b wiped out   d wiped on

7 The floral bouquets we entered into the competition were a _____ of colour, but unfortunately we didn't win first prize.

   a wham   c drop
   b riot   d buzz

8 The town coped well with the _____ of refugees.

   a interim   c input
   b inset   d influx

Grammar

Gradable & ungradable adjectives; Modifying adverbs

A Complete the sentences with the correct form of these phrases.

annoying loudness   dangerous height   immense stress   perfect cleanliness   positive glow   unbelievable charm

1 You messed up my _____ worktop with your greasy meatball sandwich!
2 Don't talk to Roberta right now; she's _____ and will bite your head off.
3 Impressed beyond measure, they gave the exquisite hotel a(n) _____ review.
4 Since they wouldn't keep it down, the manager kicked the _____ students out of the café.
5 As she was driving at a _____ speed, Martin demanded that she slow down.
6 The _____ guide convinced his group to accompany him on a risky adventure.

B Choose the correct answers.

1 This antique wardrobe cleaned up nicely; it's _____ spotless.
   a absolutely   b terribly   c slightly
2 I'm completely _____; let's take a nap.
   a sleepy   b tired   c exhausted
3 It's sad that the historical building was _____ demolished in the quake.
   a extremely   b totally   c slightly
4 The court ruled that you are _____ liable for damages.
   a a bit   b rather   c partly
5 The crowd applauded _____ after her performance.
   a entirely   b deeply   c enthusiastically
6 They asked everyone for help, but _____, they all refused.
   a miserably   b unhappily   c sadly

Hardly, barely, scarcely vs almost, virtually, practically; Position of adjectives & adverbs; Adjectives which change meaning according to their position

C Circle the correct words.

1 There were hardly / almost any survivors of the deadly plane crash; only two lived to tell their story.
2 The travel agency offered record-low rates for the package, but scarcely / virtually no one made a reservation.
3 Barely / Practically any supplies had made it to the village.
4 News was almost / scarcely published during the media blackout.
5 The tsunami practically / hardly destroyed the road leading to the remote area.
6 She had barely / almost finished reading the story to the children when the bell rang; she had to continue the next day.

D Rewrite the sentences so that the adjective follows the noun. Use two to three words.

1 Live puppies were found in the rubble.
   They found _____ in the rubble.
2 The blazing fire lasted for hours.
   The _____ for hours.
3 The ship has seven boarded passengers.
   There are seven _____ the ship.
4 The glowing patient was healthy and happy.
   The _____ with health and happiness.

E Write sentences according to the prompts.

1 people / the damage / come forward (**responsible**)
   _____

2 citizens / met / town hall (**concerned**)
   _____

3 goods / were destroyed (**damaged**)
   _____

4 belongings / the fire / replaced (**damaged**)
   _____

5 people / pay bills / time (**responsible**)
   _____

6 residents / flooding / call this number (**concerned**)
   _____

F Read the *Exam Reminder* and complete the *Exam Task*.

Exam Reminder

Referring back & forwards

- Look before and after the gaps to see if you need to use an indefinite place adverb, an indefinite pronoun, an opposite word or a repeated word to complete the gaps.
- For example, in the sentence 'Mary looked all over her bedroom for her notes, but turned up nothing', referring back to the text before 'nothing', you can deduce that she didn't find anything; in other words, she turned up 'nothing'.

Exam Task

For questions **1 – 8**, read the text below and think of the word which best fits each space. Use only **one** word in each space.

First contact

There is virtually (**1**) _____ in the world that man hasn't visited and there are (**2**) _____ cultures that he hasn't already encountered. But there are some. There are about one hundred different tribes in the world, known as uncontacted people, who have (**3**) _____ met a person from the Western world.

Most of these tribes reject contact with outsiders and one tribe in (**4**) _____, the Sentinelese, are violent towards intruders. While it's a (**5**) _____ tricky to learn about them, anthropologists do know that they have lived on North Sentinel Island for 60,000 years.

In the 1970s, a National Geographic expedition set out to film the Sentinelese; with armed policemen and a film crew in tow, they were greeted (**6**) _____ a curtain of sharp arrows and (**7**) _____ escaped alive. Further attempts to contact them were thwarted; gifts were left on the beach, but the Sentinelese launched another round of arrows, one of (**8**) _____ struck the director in the thigh. After similarly violent incidents in later years, it was concluded that the Sentinelese are to be left alone.

Listening

Exam Reminder

Choosing appropriate answers

- Ensure any verbs used in your answer choice answer the question being asked.
- Often, you will hear idiomatic expressions in the listening. Look for the answer whose response pertains to the meaning of the idiom, as opposed to a literal meaning.
- Remember that a conditional sentence or a wish can be an appropriate response if there is a hypothetical meaning in what you hear.

A Read the *Exam Reminder*. What idiom do you see in the *Exam Task* responses? Can you guess the meaning?

_____

B 7.1 ▶❙❙ Listen and complete the *Exam Task*.

Exam Task

You will hear eight questions. From three answer choices given, choose the one that best answers the question. You will hear the questions only once.

1 a The government should do something.
  b I haven't seen that wonder yet.
  c We should leave here soon.
2 a Yes, we were in a small space.
  b Yes, we barely got out of there in time.
  c Yes, they pulled some tricks on us.
3 a I've got money for a holiday.
  b I haven't got a vehicle today.
  c I've got a lot on my plate at the moment.
4 a They would never do that sort of thing.
  b Everything's been repaired, thankfully.
  c I certainly hope that's the case.

5 a What a terribly rude thing to say!
  b I'm so glad to hear that.
  c Was it not what she expected?
6 a That really was a relief.
  b The loss of life is saddening.
  c I'm glad they made it safely.
7 a We will campaign for a change in policy.
  b Raising awareness is one option.
  c They shouldn't go through with it.
8 a I'm not very hungry at the moment.
  b I'll be with you in just a minute.
  c I feel like staying in for the day.

C 7.2 ▶❙❙ Listen again and check your answers.

Writing: an essay (4)

A Read the texts and the key points. Match the key points to a text, 1 or 2. Four key points will not match either text.

Learning Reminder

Analysing complementary texts

- While reading the texts, consider if they are contrasting or complementary. Complementary texts may both have either positive or negative views about a subject, but their views essentially agree.
- Remember that each text has two key points you must summarise and evaluate, as well as including your reaction to the views expressed. Be careful not to use the same wording as in the texts – paraphrase it.
- Use a formal style and use advanced grammar to do this.

1 Making a difference a world away

For those looking for work experience and who have a desire to travel, there are few better opportunities than to volunteer abroad. It can provide experience with real-world problems while giving individuals a different perspective on life. It is even a perfect fit for those who have amassed a great deal of experience during their professional lives and who want communities in need around the globe to benefit from this.

2 Know what you are getting into

For some, volunteering abroad seems like a luxury for the young and well-off, but many agencies who find volunteers for organisations in host countries stress this does not have to be the case. These agencies can help individuals find organisations willing to pay for volunteers' travel expenses, providing they have the right skill set. They can also provide accommodation. While they do not offer a stipend, they can make sure you spend very little while you are there.

a Misconceptions about security risks ☐
b Volunteering for free room and board ☐
c The health hazards of volunteering abroad ☐
d Applying your experience where it is needed ☐
e Transport paid to work abroad as a volunteer ☐
f Aid organisation mismanagement ☐
g Getting the proper training before volunteering ☐
h Combining work and travel ☐

B Underline the words in the texts in exercise A that helped you find your answers. Which two key points from exercise A seem to provide a contrasting view?

C Read the statements and decide which texts in the *Exam Task* they relate to, 1 or 2.

1 Organisations should do their best to pick and choose the right individuals. ☐
2 There can be a clash of cultures between volunteers and management. ☐
3 Making sure the volunteers have some training can go a long way in helping them to settle into their roles. ☐
4 Volunteers should do their best to respect the way locals are running their organisation. ☐
5 An organisation tasked with rebuilding schools might prefer a volunteer who knows how to build things. ☐
6 Most volunteers have hugely different backgrounds from the local individuals who run the organisations. ☐

D Read and complete the *Exam Task* below. Don't forget to use the *Useful Expressions* on page 107 of your Student's Book.

Exam Task

Read the two texts below. Write an **essay** summarising and evaluating the key points from both texts. Use your own words throughout as far as possible, and include your own ideas in your answers.

Write your answer in 240–280 words.

1 Making an effort to fit in

While well-intentioned, international volunteers do sometimes pose challenges for local organisations. Often, the volunteers bring a different mindset with them, one that can conflict with local ideologies. They can also try to change things too fast or dominate management. Additionally, their educational level might make them feel superior to the local staff, which is not very conducive to a positive work environment.

2 Maximising potential

Volunteer organisations around the world welcome individuals from a variety of backgrounds and cultures. What's important is that they are maximising their efforts to provide the best for the local population. In some cases, organisations lack adequate vetting processes, which means they end up with inappropriately-trained personnel. Furthermore, some organisations offer little in the way of volunteer training, making it more difficult for them to assimilate into the organisation.

▶ Writing Reference p. 205 in Student's Book

Reading

A Read the *Exam Reminder*. What words from the first question of the *Exam Task* appear in multiple texts?

_____

B Now complete the *Exam Task*.

How much does a self-help book really help?

A Georgina

These days, there's a self-help book for every problem that could possibly plague our lives. By reading a self-help book, we can acquire the skills needed to cure depression, become that confident team leader at work or snare that special someone. I would say that some of these books do merit reading and there are some that I would even recommend. But a self-help book should only ever serve as a supplementary aid and never as a stand-alone cure. This is especially true if you have a recognised medical disorder, like depression, or another serious personal problem. In cases like that, you can utilise the book as a valuable resource, but make sure you're also seeing a psychologist who has got the capability of helping you.

B John

Go to the self-help section of any major bookshop and you'll be inundated with choice. It's virtually impossible to choose which one is the best, but they all claim to be on their covers! In my personal experience, I have found the information I've read in these books fascinating and they helped me – um – help myself! But let's face it – not all books are created equally. If you're in the market for one of these books, I suggest perusing online reviews before buying. And while it might take a bit of determination to put the ideas into practice successfully, it's arguably much more affordable than consulting a professional.

C Meredith

The majority of self-help books out there work on the assumption that people are able to do what a professional can do, especially when it comes to personal problems. We've all had our fair share of personal drama and, in my experience, the last thing I wanted to do was read about how to solve it. I'm sure the writers of these books are not being dishonest – they have the intention of actually helping people. However, my advice to anyone who's undergoing a personal crisis is to consult a therapist or counsellor and leave the book on the shelf.

D Sam

When it comes to searching for a way to teach yourself how to do something, whether it be how to be more productive in life, reduce feelings of intimidation or stop being so hard on yourself, there is no one-size-fits-all book. Everyone has their own way of approaching obstacles and what works for one person – or even the majority of people – doesn't necessary work for another. I believe some people are rather responsive to self-help books and gain a great deal of valuable knowledge that they're able to apply to their lives. For others, though, they have to seek help elsewhere, either from another book or another source entirely.

E Regina

One thing you'll never spot in my pocket is a self-help book. I'm terribly sceptical of the information contained within the pages. I have skimmed these sorts of books before, just out of curiosity. Maybe I'm approaching the issue in a biased way with a preconceived notion that all self-help authors are really just scam artists out to make a quick buck. But during the time I've spent in this section of the bookshop, the majority of titles I looked at sounded a bit suspect, like how to hold someone's interest at a party, get-rich-quick schemes and even one on how to buy a self-help book. Maybe I just got unlucky and came across the least helpful self-help books known to man.

You are going to read comments about self-help books. For questions **1 – 10**, choose from the people (**A – E**). The people may be chosen more than once.

Which person gives each of these opinions about self-help books?

1 The majority of individuals lack the capabilities these guides assume they have. ☐
2 A self-help book could solve one's problems and be easy on the wallet. ☐
3 Any and all obstacles in life are addressed by one self-help book or another. ☐
4 Helping oneself is a highly personalised experience. ☐
5 The merits of self-help books vary significantly from book to book. ☐
6 Many of the issues covered in these books border on the nonsensical. ☐
7 They should only ever be used in conjunction with professional guidance. ☐
8 The array of options impedes one's ability to pick the right book. ☐
9 Many are written by dishonest people merely for monetary gain. ☐
10 The tried-and-tested advice of a professional is the only way to go. ☐

Vocabulary

A **The words in bold are in the wrong sentences and of the wrong number. Write each word next to the correct sentence.**

1 The product failed the single most important **stimulus** that it was required to meet. _____

2 The **parenthesis** of all British universities must meet certain standards in order for the universities to be accredited. _____

3 Every year, the university holds a gathering in which all former **matrix** are welcome to attend. _____

4 The scientist gave the subjects random **index** to see how they would react. _____

5 The information is placed in **appendices**, as it is not terribly important and is really only supplementary. _____

6 Samantha received a very low mark for her dissertation because she had carelessly failed to include the **alumnus** at the end of the essay. _____

7 A few types of grammar **criteria** at the proficiency level are difficult for students to grasp. _____

8 The **bacteria** of books contain the page numbers of where words, topics and ideas appear for easy reference. _____

9 The data was entered into a series of **phenomenon**, which really just looked like a dizzying array of rows and columns of numbers. _____

10 Scientists have isolated the **curriculum** that causes fever from a rat bite and it looked like a piece of spiral-shaped pasta. _____

B **Complete the sentences with these words.**

> argumentative   indicative   inexplicable   infinite   intelligible   intimate   receptive   retentive

1 The professor was not _____ to questions; in fact, he answered none.

2 The universe seems to go on forever, so one would imagine there to be a(n) _____ amount of space between its non-existent borders.

3 She has _____ knowledge of gorilla behaviour, as a result of living in the Congo for a decade.

4 If you haven't got a very _____ memory, you're likely to forget the bulk of what you learn.

5 The size, shape and depth of these marks are _____ of bear claws.

6 Beth was a rather _____ student, as she frequently challenged her professor's theories in class.

7 Scientists struggled to understand what caused the _____ explosion at the reactor.

8 I can't understand what this letter says; it's not in the least bit _____.

C Circle the correct words.

1 The Roman Empire's **sphere / scope** of influence **spread / spanned** the course of several centuries.
2 Jonathan's **thesis / dissertation** statement referenced Einstein's **theory / hypothesis** of relativity.
3 On the first day of class, the professor handed out the **course / syllabus**, which indicated that students would have a busy **agenda / schedule**.
4 A detailed **criteria / analysis** suggested that the research **methodology / discipline** was deeply flawed.
5 There are charts, graphs and other **fundamental / supplementary** information in the book's **bibliography / appendix**.
6 My **statistical / scholarly** opinion is that I disagree completely with your line of **reckoning / reasoning**.
7 More than just being one of the most knowledgeable **academics / acknowledgements** at the university, Gerard was a **critical / formidable** opponent on the jousting field.
8 Given the man's lack of **insight / omen** into quantum mechanics, one can **apply / surmise** that his lecture will be pointless.

D Complete the sentences with one word in each gap.

1 I'd like to discuss our plans for exam revision, just so that we're all on the _____ page.
2 I'll explain what happened in detail, but _____ a nutshell, the dean has had to resign.
3 I'm afraid your previous courses aren't going to count _____ your degree.
4 Due to excessive socialising, Hank's responsibilities began to mount _____.
5 There are so few experiments using this theory, so it will be hard to come _____ a precedent.
6 Having finished university, Jeanne was _____ the threshold of an exciting new life abroad.
7 Don't plagiarise or you'll learn the _____ way what happens to those who do.
8 The professor hinted at the exam's extreme difficulty and students had no trouble reading between the _____.

E Read the *Exam Reminder* and complete the *Exam Task*.

Exam Reminder

Forming plural nouns
- Some gaps require plural forms, so check verb numbers and articles preceding the gaps when completing them with nouns.
- Also, make sure you are forming the plural correctly, as many do not simply add -s or -es.

Exam Task

For questions **1 – 8**, read the text below. Use the word given in capitals at the end of some of the lines to form a word that fits in the space in the same line.

Unusual degree courses

With no intention of being (1) _____ towards those universities who have compiled thoughtful, comprehensive courses in higher education, there are nevertheless some courses out there that will have you wondering about the (2) _____ behind pursuing them, even if they ultimately have something worthwhile to offer.

For example, Durham University offers a course on education studies which (3) _____ features a module on Harry Potter. Students literally engage in (4) _____ studies on the implications of casting curses and whether or not Hermione Granger was a feminist figure. Naturally, the module does not involve memorising (5) _____ full of magic spells, but rather it serves as part of a larger, more well-rounded degree. Furthermore, proponents of the module proclaim that it is beneficial to students' social skills, something employers are (6) _____ to when eyeing potential candidates.

Another such course is a contemporary circus and physical performance course at Bath University. For those who (7) _____ themselves as acrobats or other circus performers, this degree can help them attain that goal. Benefits include immersion in physical activity, critical reflection, practice in self-discipline and other (8) _____ considerations, plus the opportunity to dazzle family and friends with group and solo performances.

RESPECT
RATIONAL
EXPLAIN
ANALYSE
APPENDIX
RECEIVE
VISAGE
PHILOSOPHY

Grammar

Reporting verb patterns; Reporting suggestions; Reporting verbs followed by a gerund; Reporting questions

A Find and correct the mistakes in the verb patterns in the sentences, using no more than four words. More than one verb pattern may be possible.

1 The professor decided cancelling the exam and give everyone As. _____
2 Josie persuaded reading her uncle her dissertation and tell her what he thought. _____
3 They informed that the university its licence would be revoked. _____
4 Remind of me what units Tuesday's exam will be covering. _____
5 Did the dean propose to build a new fountain on the campus grounds? _____
6 Michael insisted to rewrite on his essay, even though it was nearly perfect. _____

B Complete the sentences with the correct form of these verbs.

agree   assure   complain   encourage   offer   suggest

1 Barney _____ studying in the auditorium the previous Wednesday.
2 He _____ to proofread my paper free of charge.
3 They _____ that they would keep the noise down while John slept.
4 My professor often _____ us to do peer reviews of our assignments.
5 They _____ that they didn't have enough time to complete the exam.
6 My parents _____ me that they'd help me out with expenses at university.

C Write sentences using the Past Simple for reporting verbs and any other words you may need.

1 Bill / deny / cheat / exam

_____

2 Sue / congratulate / Neil / graduate

_____

3 they / apologise / be late

_____

4 Sean / inquire / graduate programme

_____

5 Kelly / describe / events / Sheila

_____

6 they / state / funds / delay

_____

D Circle the correct words.

1 The teaching assistant asked **if / whether** or not she had to mark all the papers by Friday.
2 The dean questioned **his / if** using a paid service to write the paper.
3 Dana categorically **admitted / denied** stealing exam papers prior to being examined.
4 Professor Burns didn't waste time wondering **how / who** every student in his class got the same mark.
5 Helen suspected **to use / using** Jill's notes as a study guide would be a mistake.
6 The two science geniuses continually argue **with / over** whose theory was best.
7 Paul expressed an interest **to enrol / in enrolling** in post-graduate studies.
8 Byron asked **if / where** George had left his microbiology thesis on a public computer.

E Read the *Exam Reminder* and complete the *Exam Task.*

Exam Task

Read the passage about plagiarism, then choose the word or phrase that best completes the sentence.

Paying the price for stealing others' words

When it comes to plagiarism, professors repeatedly warn students (1) _____ doing it; nonetheless, there are a number of cases in British universities every year. In some, a university's advisory board (2) _____ that the student's marks for a module be dropped to zero, which has serious ramifications for their degree. Students (3) _____ of two things: that the punishment is too harsh and that they were (4) _____ informed of the rules. But are students correct in (5) _____ that it's the university's responsibility to explain (6) _____ the rules concerning plagiarism? Oughtn't they just automatically know that they should never copy other people's work?

But officials have seen a steep rise in the number of students (7) _____ of plagiarising written assignments, so they have been forced to (8) _____ that perhaps students don't even realise what plagiarism is. Many websites offer 'free essays' that students think they can just copy and paste and use how they like. Still, it begs the question: do students really need to be explicitly told not to copy materials from the internet? It seems like a no-brainer.

	a		b		c		d	
1	over		not		against		to	
2	promises		recommends		mentions		offers	
3	criticise		protest		complain		object	
4	–		yet		never		also	
5	reminding		persuading		suggesting		convincing	
6	about		that		them		–	
7	accused		denied		blamed		charged	
8	admit		announce		describe		tell	

Checking verb patterns

- Learn what parts of speech follow what verbs and check that the pattern is correct in your answer.
- Remember that some gaps will require a verb with a negative meaning. Read the sentence carefully to decide if a positive or negative verb meaning is needed.
- Be careful that you haven't chosen a pattern that is correct in your own language, but not in English.

Listening

A Read the *Exam Reminder*. In which gap(s) of the *Exam Task* might you need to use a possessive case?

_____

B 8.1 ▶ Listen and complete the *Exam Task.*

Exam Reminder

Writing grammatically correct structures

- Remember to check that your answers fit in with the grammar of the sentence. Make sure that the spelling is correct and that there are apostrophes, if necessary.
- Be careful to write only one answer in the gap; writing two answers means you will get no marks at all.
- Write only what is necessary to answer the question and write your answers in capital letters on the answer sheet.

Exam Task

You will hear an instructor talking about a new teaching methodology called a flipped classroom. For questions **1 – 8**, complete the sentences with a word or short phrase.

1 The speaker says the _____ support for his idea was rather weak.

2 His new teaching methodology reflected _____ that other professors had published.

3 The speaker believes it needed _____ to convince those in power of the efficacy of the methodology.

4 Problem schools are described by the speaker as having extremely high _____.

5 It was a _____ who went on to create a school which employed the use of recorded lectures.

6 In a traditional classroom, the _____ occurs during the in-class lesson.

7 The speaker says he spends just a little time on the _____ information nowadays.

8 The speaker thinks one drawback could be some students' lack of _____ regarding watching the videos.

C 8.2 ▶ Listen again and check your answers.

Writing: a report (1)

A Decide if the statements are facts (F), evaluations (E) or recommendations (R).

1 It would be highly advisable to place young learners in day care environments that provide learning opportunities. ☐

2 All of the activities at the learning centre are both entertaining and thought-provoking. ☐

3 There are a number of interactive games the children can play with, which also double as learning devices. ☐

4 It is recommended that working mums and dads in need of day care should consider a programme like ours. ☐

5 Children are encouraged to work together, which fosters their teamworking abilities. ☐

Learning Reminder

Understanding the content of a report

• Remember that reports are factual in nature, include descriptions and are neutral in tone, and the target audience is a peer group or a superior.

• Provide headings for your reports and include clear introductory sentences for each paragraph.

• Use language that is appropriate for describing, comparing, analysing and recommending.

B Read these partial task prompts and answer the questions.

Task 1: You recently attended a meeting with a publisher of educational materials. Your company would like a report describing the components being offered, the quality of the materials and the target age range.

Task 2: You recently worked as a volunteer for a group that builds schools for the poor. You have been asked to write a report describing the activities you undertook, how organised the group was and the expertise of the building team.

Task 3: You've recently reviewed a new placement test for a language school you work for. Write a report describing the sections and task types of the test, and evaluate its effectiveness in placing students in appropriate language levels.

a Who are the target audiences in each of these reports?

b Excluding introductions and conclusions, what headings would you use in each of these reports?

c In which tasks, 1, 2 or 3 would you use the following vocabulary?

reading comprehension ☐	adolescent learners ☐	teacher's resource pack ☐
not very knowledgeable ☐	misassigned candidates ☐	multimedia components ☐
fresh, engaging content ☐	grammar companion ☐	disorganised management ☐

C Replace words and phrases in the sections of a report with these words and phrases which elevate the language to a more formal level. What headings would you assign to these sections?

are sensitive to   arithmetic   audio stimuli   constructive   content   labelled photography   lyrics
personal attention from   pride ourselves on   special bonds   suitable   visual stimuli

———————————
The learning content is great for nursery school children, as it teaches them basic maths and spelling skills. There is a mix of sights, such as pictures with words, and sounds, such as music that teaches through words, which helps all children.

———————————
The learning environment is helpful and all of the teachers care about the children's needs. Each child gets one-on-one time with teachers on a daily basis and we are proud of ourselves for forming friendships with children that make them feel happy.

D Read and complete the *Exam Task* below. Don't forget to use the *Useful Expressions* on page 121 of your Student's Book.

Exam Task

You are a teacher at a facility called First Steps Day Care. Your supervisor has asked you to write a report evaluating the facility's nursery school education programme. You must describe the programme and evaluate its content, the learning environment and the activities children engage in. You should also assess the course's benefits for parents who wish to enrol their children and give any recommendations.

Write your **report** in 280–320 words.

↪ Writing Reference p. 208 in Student's Book

Vocabulary

A Choose the correct answers.

1 The essay draws a(n) _____ contrast between life before and after the Industrial Revolution.

a severe   b edgy

c bitter   d sharp

2 Don't forget to _____ your sources; you don't want to get accused of stealing information.

a quote   b cite

c name   d refer

3 You could spend a whole day exploring Paris and it would still be a _____ in the ocean for what the city has to offer.

a dip   b drip

c drop   d drag

4 Josie spent 14 months _____ all the information for her dissertation.

a commending   b conducting

c compiling   d condoning

5 I enjoy my physics course because my professor is so _____ to questions.

a retentive   b respective

c receptive   d repetitive

6 People who don't ever want to travel anywhere could be accused of being _____.

a cold-hearted   b quick-witted

c sharp-tongued   d narrow-minded

7 She had never considered going to Thailand before; she travelled there on a _____.

a whim   b wham

c whine   d while

8 The list of the sources for the information in this book is contained in the book's _____.

a periodical   b acknowledgements

c appendix   d bibliography

9 The man the police were looking for _____ off in the other direction.

a tailed   b headed

c backed   d tracked

10 The tourist centre has had a recent _____ of visitors from Russia.

a invasion   b influx

c infiltration   d incursion

11 I'm upset; the courses I took two years ago aren't going to _____ towards my degree.

a amount   b number

c count   d measure

12 Crimes such as robberies and muggings were completely _____ of in that area.

a disregarded   b unheard

c overlooked   d misunderstood

13 Travelling to Norway and experiencing the Northern Lights first hand was always at the very top of Mary's _____ list.

a luggage   b lag

c basket   d bucket

14 I can't understand why this experiment failed; it's _____.

a inhospitable   b unintelligible

c inexplicable   d unremarkable

15 Larry was an experienced gardener, but some aspects of botany went beyond the _____ of his expertise.

a scope   b sphere

c span   d spectrum

16 This machinery is complex and rather demanding; it'll take you some time to learn the _____.

a lines   b cords

c ropes   d cables

17 I never would have thought the board would come _____ to your idea – how did you convince them?

a into   b by

c round   d over

18 The management team had lots to say about your proposal, but _____ a nutshell, you've got the job.

a at   b on

c in   d to

19 Copy someone's work, online or otherwise, and your _____ can and should be exposed!

a methodology   b plagiarism

c hypothesis   d discipline

20 I don't want to go on some boring guided tour; let's do something adventurous and go off the beaten _____.

a lane   b track

c route   d trail

Grammar

B Choose the correct answers.

1. Mary finally decided _____ a topic for her final dissertation.

   a to   **b** –

   c on   **d** that

2. The city's a ghost town; _____ no one was out on the streets.

   a hardly   **b** scarcely

   c barely   **d** virtually

3. The mayor assured _____ the convention centre would be built on time.

   a to   **b** that them

   c them that   **d** –

4. Leslie _____ to put in some extra hours to finish the work on time.

   a advised   **b** offered

   c suggested   **d** recommended

5. The coach congratulated _____ their stunning win in the final.

   a on the team   **b** on

   c the team on   **d** the team

6. The council _____ us that we would not be reimbursed for our losses.

   a informed   **b** said

   c reported   **d** let

7. She was _____ devastated by damage to her home during the floods.

   a slightly   **b** moderately

   c absolutely   **d** rarely

8. He was accused _____ a number of crimes, included shoplifting and defacing property.

   a by   **b** of

   c –   **d** on

9. Martin apologised _____ mango juice all over his guest's white coat.

   a to spilling   **b** for spilling

   c by spilling   **d** to spill

10. Lynn asked _____ or not Henry could help her move house on Sunday.

    a if   **b** whether

    c when   **d** how

11. She _____ the policeman's right to enter the property without a signed warrant.

    a examined   **b** calculated

    c inquired   **d** questioned

12. Paula's parents proposed _____ her to a local, less expensive university.

    a of sending   **b** sending

    c send   **d** to sending

13. He was _____ upset that the project was experiencing a delay.

    a narrowly   **b** scarcely

    c somewhat   **d** just

14. I'm in the market for a _____ priced vehicle; nothing too expensive nor too cheap.

    a reasonably   **b** dramatically

    c surprisingly   **d** simply

15. The heatwave was so intense, _____ anyone wasn't affected in some way.

    a practically   **b** virtually

    c scarcely   **d** utterly

16. Although I don't get paid for volunteering, I find the job to be _____ rewarding.

    a greatly   **b** partially

    c hugely   **d** perfectly

17. They _____ about the property across the street to see if it was affordably priced.

    a insisted   **b** inquired

    c mentioned   **d** reminded

18. Could I get a show of hands from the _____ at yesterday's meeting?

    a present students   **b** students presently

    c students present   **d** presently students

19. Having been playing for hours outside, the team _____ their pizza.

    a hungry devoured   **b** devoured hungrily

    c devoured hungry   **d** hungrily devoured

20. Parents get angry with children sometimes, but a _____ will explain to their children why they can or cannot do something.

    a parent responsibly   **b** parent responsible

    c responsibly parent   **d** responsible parent

Review 4 — Units 7 & 8

Use of English

C Read the text below and decide which answer (a, b, c or d) best fits each gap.

A marvel of research

Postgraduate students occasionally write (1) _____ on rather bizarre topics. Some might seem (2) _____ ridiculous to the casual onlooker and it's anyone's guess as to the researcher's (3) _____ behind exploring such a topic. One studies jumping height differences between cat fleas and dog fleas, another (4) _____ that mosquitoes may be more attracted to Limburger cheese than humans are and a third gives a(n) (5) _____ of the dangers of sword swallowing. In terms of the study of life, mankind leaves no stone unturned.

A perhaps more useful but still unusual subject was published by a researcher at University College London. An authority (6) _____ neuroscience, Eleanor Maguire studied the brains of London's black cab drivers. Having to memorise routes along more than 25,000 streets, a cabbie of the British capital has anything (7) _____ a poor memory. Maguire learned that these (8) _____ drivers have larger posterior hippocampi – the part of the brain responsible for spatial memory. This serves as proof that a brain is like a muscle and it's imperative that we flex it.

	a	**b**	**c**	**d**
1	agendas	syllabuses	dissertations	assignments
2	barely	utterly	slightly	reasonably
3	motive	apparatus	scope	thesis
4	reasons	rationalises	surmises	hypothesises
5	analysis	review	argument	acknowledgement
6	with	to	in	on
7	of	but	for	not
8	assiduous	invasive	intelligible	inexplicable

D Complete the sentences with the correct form of the words in bold.

1	Nancy moulded the clay into a _____ shape.	**SPHERE**
2	I was wondering if you had any _____ into the resolution of this dilemma.	**SIGHT**
3	Clara is a rather _____ child for her age.	**INQUIRE**
4	Michael asked the astronomer if he had seen any space _____ through his telescope.	**ODD**
5	The head of the board was the person with the _____ vote in all matters.	**DECIDE**
6	Although they say there is a border, the universe seems as if it goes on _____.	**FINITE**
7	If you see an owl in a forest, it is believed to be an _____ sign.	**OMEN**
8	The book is rich with data, all of which is referenced in the three _____.	**APPENDIX**

E Complete the text with one word in each gap.

Teaching abroad

Many native English speakers use their knowledge of the language to head **(1)** _____ to foreign lands and teach. Few can do this on a **(2)** _____, of course, for it takes planning as well as teacher training. To be successful at teaching a language, it's **(3)** _____ enough to just be fluent. Students insist **(4)** _____ detailed explanations of grammatical structures but, the truth is, most native speakers can't readily explain **(5)** _____ a mixed conditional is formed, let alone its meaning. But with an intensive course in lesson planning, applied linguistics and a thirst for knowledge, the savvy ones catch **(6)** _____ quickly. Asked **(7)** _____ or not the journey lived up to their expectations, practically **(8)** _____ teacher would say it went according to plan; while rewarding, both teaching and being immersed in a new culture can be a challenge to one's soul.

F Complete the second sentence so that it has a similar meaning to the first sentence, using the word given. Do not change the word given. You must use between three and eight words, including the word given.

1 Almost no trees were left standing after the tornado.
   barely
   Because of the tornado, _____ left standing.

2 People who attended the conference were given free materials.
   present
   Free _____ conference.

3 The employees received a warning from the manager about being late.
   warned
   The manager _____ late.

4 They said Jill told lies to the group.
   accused
   Jill _____ the group.

5 The soldiers put up a valiant fight on the field.
   valiantly
   The _____ on the field.

6 Paul was asked if he was ready to compete.
   not
   They _____ ready to compete.

Reading

A Read the *Exam Reminder*. Which questions in the *Exam Task* ask you about the definition of a word or phrase?

_____

B Now complete the *Exam Task*.

Exam Reminder

Determining the meaning of specific words

- Sometimes you are asked about the meaning of a word or phrase in a text. If you are unsure of its meaning, read the sentence it is in, as well as the sentences before and after it.
- When you have decided on an answer, check that the other choices do not fit within the context of the sentence, to ensure you have made the right decision.

1

Staying in the nest

Leaving the nest might be a traditional rite of passage, but trends demonstrate that young adults must be entering adulthood through some other doorway, as more and more of them remain living with their parents, even into their thirties. A recent study on social trends attempts to answer questions about why the nest has become so hard to leave.

A variety of reasons are attributable to the fact that, in the last 15 years in the UK, there has been an increase of around 300,000 young adults staying with their mum and dad. One is that many more young people are enrolling at university, a circumstance which makes juggling the added burdens of utility bills and tuition fees impossible on one's own. The difficulties don't cease once students graduate either, because most end up saddled with debt due to soaring expenses.

A further look at the figures reveals a more telling account of why more are staying put ... housing in the UK is simply unaffordable whether you enter higher education or go directly into the workforce. A runaway housing market has caused a spike in house prices and demand for living space has sent rents through the roof as well. Forty-four per cent – nearly half of all surveyed 15 to 30-year-olds in Britain – complained that housing costs weighed heavily on their decision to delay leaving home. Interestingly enough, 12 per cent stated that the comforts of home were too sweet a deal to give up.

Coupled with the rise in nest-stayers is singledom. The number of marriages being recorded annually in the past few years is as low as it was in 1895 and the average age for individuals' first-time marriage has jumped by almost two years since 1996. Additionally, women are on average four years older at the birth of their first child than they were in 1971. While researchers haven't determined if the unaffordability of leaving the nest has attributed to these changes, or if it's just a personal choice among the youth of today, it is noted that living at home has become much easier due to the generation gap being less of an issue. As such, adult children feel more comfortable around their parents than they used to, which means that, for whatever reason, this changing trend is not causing much additional friction between the parties involved.

2

A bed-living-bath-cooking-dining room

Demand for living space in London has reached epic proportions and laws enacted to protect renters from unscrupulous landlords have barely made a dent in providing a reasonable quality of life in the British capital. The latest housing act is a perfect example of lawmakers' indifference towards the subject; the minimum space requirement for renting a studio flat is set at 110 square feet for two adult tenants and at 70 square feet for a single occupant. And be prepared to fork out upwards of 1,000 pounds a month for this 'shoebox' of a home that campaigners against the act label 'rabbit hutch properties'.

This, of course, is not the label used by landlords advertising the space. A 'dynamic studio flat' turns out to be a unit of less than 88 square feet, an 'eat-in kitchen area' describes a room which is both a kitchen and a shower, and 'mezzanine sleeping gallery' translates to a bed that's more or less hung from the ceiling. The descriptions also fail to mention the appalling conditions of the exorbitantly priced rentals.

Most of these studios – or 'semi' studios – are part of what was once a larger, normal-sized flat. The modus operandi is this: the owner of the flat will have it 're-sectioned' and rent out every single room in the flat as a separate semi-studio, in order to maximise profits. Almost no room in a flat is spared; thus, not only do bedrooms, living rooms and dining rooms become self-contained bedsits with tiny cooking areas, but so does the kitchen. In one such case, the landlord didn't even bother to remove the cupboards from the kitchen, so it was obvious which of the half a dozen semi-studios in the flat was once the kitchen of the main flat.

As useful as the housing act can be, raising the legal minimum size of habitations is only one step in stemming the tide of 'rabbit hutch properties' entering the market each year, which one study states is 20,000 annually in London alone. What would go further in remedying this crisis would be to build more housing to accommodate demand. Sadly, as more individuals flood the city looking for a place to stay near their work, a revolt against renting these types of properties altogether seems unlikely.

Read the two passages from a scientific magazine, then answer the questions according to the information given in each passage.

Text 1

1 What is the main purpose of this passage?
  a to provide solutions to a problem
  b to explain a changing situation
  c to report on worrying trends
  d to outline a history of trends

2 In the second sentence of paragraph 2, which of these words could replace **juggling**?
  a avoiding
  c paying
  b moving
  d managing

3 Which reason is a secondary cause of young people staying at home into adulthood?
  a obtaining higher education
  b rising costs of housing
  c tendencies to remain unmarried
  d comforts afforded in the home

4 Why does the author mention the rise in the average marrying age?
  a to establish a connection with other factors
  b to report on another changing trend
  c to describe a worry among young people's parents
  d to discuss a result of changing personal choices

Text 2

5 How can the author's attitude throughout the article best be described?
  a indignant
  c indifferent
  b complacent
  d puzzled

6 Which of the following has resulted from the housing act described in the passage?
  a caps on maximum amounts of monthly rent
  b standards of cleanliness for living quarters
  c guaranteed minimum amount of space per flat
  d straightforward reporting of rental adverts

7 In the second sentence of paragraph 3, how would you define **modus operandi**?
  a a usual way of doing things
  b a type of rental agreement
  c a dishonest landlord
  d a legal requirement

8 What solution does the author suggest for improving the situation?
  a It is a matter of implementing stricter laws.
  b Renters must shun semi-studios, forcing a change.
  c Simply building more homes will solve the crisis.
  d A two-pronged solution is necessary.

Vocabulary

A Circle the correct words.

1 The landlord / tenant is asking for the rent; it was due two weeks ago!
2 The kingdom had no intention of participating in a regional war and remained neutral / sovereign.
3 Let's dismiss / dispense with the pleasantries and get down to business, shall we?
4 Catalonia is a(n) autonomous / liberated region of Spain, meaning it largely governs itself but it must still adhere to Spanish law.
5 To rent this flat, you must provide a list of utilities / references so that your past payment history can be checked.
6 It's a spacious office, so spend some time obligating / orientating yourself so that you know where everything is.
7 I'm being called away on business for six months and I would like to sublet / let my flat so that I'm not paying rent for a place I'm not living in.
8 Foreigners are often not emancipated / enfranchised to vote in the elections of their host country.

B Complete the sentences with the correct form of the words in bold.

1 South Sudan gained its _____ from Sudan in 2011. **DEPEND**
2 The _____ notice states that you have ten days to vacate the property. **EVICT**
3 Even though he was merely renting it, Henry has a sense of _____ to his flat that made him believe he could do what he wanted with it. **TITLE**
4 When asked how the party was, Kelly smiled faintly and gave the _____ answer. **OBLIGATE**
5 Mel was _____ so she sat down for a minute to collect her thoughts. **ORIENTATE**
6 Jeff wasn't very sensitive to his employees' needs and was often _____ of them. **DISMISS**
7 Louis's supreme _____ was on display when he tossed a pile of paperwork up into the air and stormed out of his office. **MATURE**
8 No one down here makes workplace decisions; they're all made _____. **HIERARCHY**

C Complete the sentences using these words.

fend   lift   pull   settle   stand   step   strike   tend

1 After it was revealed that the executive lied on his CV, he was asked to _____ down from his post.
2 Helen managed to _____ out on her own after years with the agency.
3 Don't be so dramatic; just _____ down and pull yourself together.
4 Mary broke her ankle, so could you _____ in for her at Saturday night's performance?
5 I can't give you any more help on this project; I'm afraid you're just going to have to _____ for yourself.
6 If you can't _____ your own weight around here, they're likely to find a replacement.
7 Don't waste your time asking Tom for assistance; he won't _____ a finger to help you.
8 I suggest you _____ to all your affairs before you decide to take a leave of absence from work.

D Complete the text with one word in each gap.

Some simple wisdom

Being an adult means more than just being grown (1) _____, but showing that you can make responsible decisions. Here are some examples of irresponsible behaviour in the context of work.

An employee who's continually saddled (2) _____ frustrating tasks at work storms into their boss's office and hands (3) _____ their resignation. On top of that, they've got no money saved and no other job lined up. It sets off a chain of events in which they wind up flat broke, fall (4) _____ on their rent and have to lean (5) _____ parents or friends for support.

Conversely, an employee who's bored at work, constantly misses deadlines, and is generally unhappy and unpleasant to be around can be given their walking (6) _____ or, if there's a downturn in the company, wind up laid (7) _____, as no employer would want to keep such an ineffective member of staff on board.

The responsible reaction is this: realise the situation you're in and do something about it – rationally! Either talk to your boss about the work you're being given and the effect it's having on you, or line another job up and resign (8) _____ your post in a calm, respectable manner. In the end, you'll be very proud of yourself for handling it this way.

Exam Reminder

Dealing with idioms & expressions.

• Try to think of what word completes the idiom or expression before you look at the choices. If you do not know the idiom, look at the choices to see if one sounds plausible.

• If you are still unsure, think about other phrases you know which mean something similar and identify if any of the words used in the answer options are the same.

E Read the *Exam Reminder* and complete the *Exam Task*.

Exam Task

Choose the word or phrase that best completes the sentence.

1 Margaret will be on _____ leave for several months after the baby is born.
   a parenthood   c motherhood
   b paternity   d maternity

2 Companies are required to pay _____ for hourly employees who work more than 40 hours per week.
   a overtime   c downtime
   b flexitime   d sometime

3 If you decide to take early _____, you may find that your pension will be much lower.
   a resignation   c retirement
   b release   d retreat

4 I'm here to _____ my resignation because I've found a better-paying job elsewhere.
   a submit   c hand
   b propose   d tender

5 Susie doesn't do a whole lot of work around the office because she's very good at _____ her duties.
   a delegating   c entrusting
   b assigning   d committing

6 This job doesn't require a lot of high-level skills as it's mostly _____ labour.
   a bodily   c brute
   b manual   d unrefined

7 The _____ costs I had to pay for this flat meant I had to save up for four months.
   a rising   c forward
   b start-up   d upfront

8 The disgruntled employee was _____ from the property by force.
   a confiscated   c eradicated
   b eliminated   d removed

Grammar

Relative Clauses; Relative pronouns with quantifiers; Replacing relative clauses with participle clauses; Clauses of reason, purpose, result & contrast; Other uses of participle clauses

A Complete the second sentence so that it has a similar meaning to the first sentence. Use relative pronouns and any other words you might need.

1 The students repeated the words they heard on the recording.
The students repeated _____ they heard on the recording.

2 All six tenants were evicted for not paying rent.
All six tenants, _____ were paying rent, were evicted.

3 Jim now takes the bus because his car was written off.
Jim, _____ was written off, now takes the bus.

4 He only has two decent suits and they're dirty.
He only has two decent suits, _____ are dirty.

B Circle the correct word in the second sentence so that it matches the meaning in the first sentence.

1 The positions, which are entry level, don't pay well.
All / Some of the positions are entry level and don't pay well.

2 The staff who are bilingual can assist with calls abroad.
A few / All of the staff are bilingual and can assist with calls abroad.

3 The entrants who applied in June will be seen first.
All / A number of the entrants applied in June and will be seen first.

4 The car, which was manufactured last year, had defects.
Every / One car manufactured last year had defects.

C Complete the sentences with the correct form of these verbs. Use only one word in each gap.

claim   complete   line   participate   suffer

1 Athletes _____ in next month's marathon should register with organisers as soon as possible.

2 Any belongings not _____ after six weeks will be thrown out.

3 Kids _____ from online abuse should tell their parents immediately.

4 Transactions _____ before 2pm will appear on your account today.

5 The buildings _____ the cliff's edge were condemned due to structural damage.

D Complete the clauses with appropriate linking phrases according to the prompts. More than one answer may be possible.

1 Jim cut down the tree in his garden _____ have a view of the surrounding countryside. (**purpose**)

2 _____ Barb dislikes living in the city, she does so for work. (**contrast**)

3 _____ so many candidates vying for posts, the job market has become fiercely competitive. (**reason**)

4 Coffee was spilt all over my CV, _____ I had to reprint it. (**result**)

5 Helen wears ear plugs at night _____ hear the noise coming from the street. (**purpose**)

E Choose the correct answer.

Exam Task

Natalie, (**1**) _____ last year of university was fast approaching, had some difficult choices to make. She wished to stay in her university town, with friends nearby. But (**2**) _____ few work prospects there, she would in effect be sacrificing her career. The high-tech firms (**3**) ____ in the area were small and had little to offer her, not that she would have passed up a less ambitious post (**4**) ____ hold onto her comfortable life. (**5**) ____ at every one and received no response, Natalie's sinking feeling grew as each day passed. (**6**) ____ she hated the idea of relocating, she knew it was inevitable. Then she saw a job advert that turned her frown upside down …

1 a who	b whose	c which	d whom
2 a what	b what with	c so as not to	d in view of
3 a establishing	b established	c establish	d in establishing
4 a in order to	b because of	c in	d so
5 a Having	b Having been applied	c Having applied	d Applying
6 a Much as	b So as to	c Because	d However

F Read the *Exam Reminder* and complete the *Exam Task*.

Exam Task

For questions **1 – 5**, complete the second sentence so that it has a similar meaning to the first sentence, using the word given. **Do not change the word given.** You must use between **three** and **eight** words, including the word given.

1 To make a good impression, Paula bought a new suit.

   as

   Paula bought a new suit _____ bad impression.

2 I was visited by my new neighbours yesterday and one is from South Africa.

   of

   My _____ South Africa, visited me yesterday.

3 The contractors were paid so that the work could be finished.

   order

   They paid _____ the work.

4 They were informed of the leaky ceiling when they signed the lease.

   having

   After _____ the leaky ceiling.

5 The man who is on the other side of the fence damaged the postbox.

   standing

   The postbox was damaged by the _____ fence.

Exam Reminder

Writing the correct number of words

- The maximum number of words you can write is eight, so if your answer is too long, try to make it shorter, or check that it is correct.
- When you have completed the second sentence, check the first sentence again to make sure you have not written any unnecessary words.

Listening

A Read the *Exam Reminder*. In which question in the *Exam Task* will you compare what two people have said?

_____

Exam Reminder

Writing short notes

- Making notes is important if you only hear the talk once, so be sure to read the questions carefully so that you will know what information to make a note of while listening.
- Try to infer meaning from the context, as ideas are often implied rather than stated directly.

B 🔊 9.1 ▶️ Listen and complete the *Exam Task*.

Exam Task

You will hear three short segments from a radio programme. You will hear what three different radio guests have to say about three different topics. After each talk, you will be asked some questions. From the three answer choices given, you should choose the one that best answers the question according to the information you heard.

Segment One

1 What's the woman's attitude concerning internships?

   a They are demanding but worthwhile for individuals.

   b Their benefits have been very much ruined by companies.

   c They should be avoided and done away with entirely.

2 Regarding the type of abuse the man suggests interns receive, the woman elaborates on

   a having to work long hours.

   b doing useless, demeaning tasks.

   c being misled by potential employees.

Segment Two

3 How does the man describe his experience of learning his rights?

   a He describes it as being very thorough.

   b He believes everyone should go through it.

   c He wishes it had happened in some other way.

4 Which actions occurred swiftly?

   a refusing to respond to renters' requests and posting the eviction notice

   b posting the eviction notice and getting the deposit back

   c noticing leaks and noises and seeking legal counsel

Segment Three

5 What does the woman imply about office work?

   a There is a lack of freedom in this environment.

   b Anyone who's done it knows how restrictive it is.

   c The constraints of the office are only in our minds.

6 The woman characterises being your own boss and paying for your own services as

   a impossible feats for most individuals.

   b the very least of one's worries.

   c the reason for keeping many contacts.

C 🔊 9.2 ▶️ Listen again and check your answers.

Writing: an article (2)

Learning Reminder

A Decide if the sentences would appear in an article (A) or essay (E). Then match these functions to the sentences.

analysis   anecdote   argument   description   narration   persuasion

How articles differ from essays
- While articles can be either serious or lively in tone, essays are more academic and factual.
- Depending on the audience, an article can include personal stories, narration and descriptions. If the article is for an academic journal, however, it will have a different, more formal and factual style.
- Articles intend to describe, whereas essays intend to persuade, and include analyses, statistics and the writer's opinion or recommendation.

1 Financial institutions have an obligation to assist small businesses; without this support, many would never get off the ground, further harming the economy. ☐ _____

2 Having a business partner can help with start-up costs, but it also means that both business partners will have to make joint decisions, which can lead to disagreements. ☐ _____

3 You have to deal with the public, who can be very inquisitive, friendly and engaging, but who can also complain. ☐ _____

4 I remember once when the server I use for my business crashed and I had to scramble to get someone in to fix it. ☐ _____

5 The results of the survey show that businesses succeed when they provide a product the market needs and when staff is flexible to changing business climates. ☐ _____

6 Do you picture yourself selling your arts and crafts at a stand in a busy commercial area of town to passers-by? ☐ _____

B The notes are aspects of starting a new business. Match the sentences (1–8) to the aspects they develop. Then decide if the sentences are anecdotes (A), descriptions (D) or narration (N).

finding the financial backing ☐☐   having a strong character ☐☐

forming partnerships with friends ☐☐   planning out your business ☐☐

1 Just remember that if you choose to do this, you'll have to run everything by your partner; you can't make unilateral decisions. ☐

2 You'll have to be responsible; you may have to burn the midnight oil in the beginning until you get the hang of it. ☐

3 I was fortunate enough to get assistance from my parents, who helped me obtain a small business loan. ☐

4 I set up my business online, with photos of my work and a smooth, prompt delivery service. ☐

5 We had known one another for several years, were like-minded people and had already worked through our fair share of arguments. ☐

6 Is there something you're good at making, such as jewellery or T-shirt designs? ☐

7 How you handle your business challenges will be instrumental in the success – or failure – of the enterprise. ☐

8 When I first set foot in the bank, I suddenly had a sick feeling – what if they don't approve my application? ☐

C Read the partial paragraphs from articles about starting a new business and complete them with a sentence (1–8) from exercise B. Which aspect from exercise B does each paragraph develop?

1 You have to conjure up a good idea, if you haven't already done so. ☐ In my case it was the latter and, thankfully, I knew artists who could draw the designs I wanted.

2 ☐ I remember once when the server I use for my business crashed and I had to scramble to get someone in to fix it. We were up very late into the night making sure it was fully functional and back in service.

D Read and complete the *Exam Task*.
Don't forget to use the *Useful Expressions* on page 137 of your Student's Book.

↻ Writing Reference p. 207 in Student's Book

Exam Task

A lifestyle magazine has asked readers to send in articles on the topic of young entrepreneurs. You decide to write an article in which you describe how to start a business. You should explain two important aspects young entrepreneurs should know before they get started, using your own ideas and personal experiences.

Write your **article** in 280–320 words.

Reading

A Read the *Exam Reminder*. Which missing paragraphs in the *Exam Task* could feasibly answer the first gap based on the first sentences alone?

_____

B Now complete the *Exam Task*.

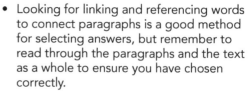

The origins of advertising

Advertising has become a major force in our modern world. Through our airwaves, up in the skies, on walls, streets and along motorways, almost nowhere can we go and not be bombarded by adverts. It has become so prevalent that scientists and researchers have analysed its sociological effect extensively – how it influences buying habits, desensitises consumers and in some cases even repels them. **1** ☐

Such rudimentary content is also believed to be present in the first printed adverts, used by ancient Egyptians to communicate sales messages through the use of papyrus. In contrast with the ephemeral nature of today's advertising, they would also carve messages of commerce into stone or on steel plates, which would remain visible for a lifetime. **2** ☐

Naturally, we cannot know for sure, but one would guess that the power of persuasion was present in the spoken adverts of ancient times. You could suppose that the loudest, most colourful, most entertaining crier garnered the most business. Although we do not experience this form of advertisement often today, sellers in public markets in Europe and the Middle East still employ this method. **3** ☐

The specific message on the printing plate was 'We buy high quality steel rods and make fine quality needles, to be ready for use at home in no time', and the seller also placed a rabbit logo and the name of his shop in the centre. The plate, made of copper and dating back to the Song dynasty of 10th-century China, was used to print posters, the dimensions of which were nearly perfect squares roughly the size of a window frame. **4** ☐

It was not until the rise of newspapers did advertising make its next big leap. During this time, targeted slogans and catchphrases became popular. The first such instance of a paid newspaper advert appeared in the French newspaper *La Presse* in 1836 and what was so revolutionary about it was that the seller paid for its placement, allowing the newspaper to charge its readers less. **5** ☐

Known as 'quackery', such messages boasted cures for common ailments that went above and beyond what traditional remedies could provide. Naturally, an unsuspecting and undereducated public was particularly susceptible to such fabrications. Much as how quackery would be dispelled today, doctors went out of their way to publish medical journals debunking the claims made by these adverts. **6** ☐

In the advert, a painting of a child blowing bubbles – a work of art literally entitled *Bubbles*, by English artist Sir John Everett Millais – was used as the background of a poster, with the product visible in the foreground. The visual immediately linked the product with high-class society and it is a tactic that is undeniably still very much used today. **7** ☐

Along with the staggering investment is the use of a broad range of tactics to maximise impact, such as focus groups, evocative imagery, storytelling and seemingly boundless product placement. So psychological is the effect that it has given rise to the belief that companies know everything about you. Nevertheless, with such creativity poured into the field, one can still appreciate its art form and its place in history.

You are going to read an extract from an article. Seven paragraphs have been removed from the extract. Choose from the paragraphs **A – H** the one which fits each gap (**1 – 7**). There is one extra paragraph which you do not need to use.

A One need look no further than failed advertising campaigns. Some went too far in their shock value, had to be apologised for and hurt the brand more than they helped. In one example, a game manufacturer, in order to promote the carnal violence visible in the game, held an event which showcased an actual deceased goat.

B For better or worse, there was no stopping the budding advertising industry. Agencies started to spring up and with that came campaigns. The first successful campaign was for the British soap manufacturer Pears. With the help of chairman Thomas James Barratt, the company successfully linked a catchy slogan with high culture.

C In contrast to the adverts being produced for the literate populace of this region, text was largely absent from adverts that proliferated in the towns and cities of medieval Europe. To circumvent this obstacle, adverts used commonly recognisable imagery such as a boot for a cobbler or a diamond for a carver to promote products and services. And still, criers remained the go-to medium for relaying the sellers' messages to the public.

D Also entering the industry was the vast sums of money that companies would splash out on campaigns. A little over one hundred American companies in 1893 spent 50,000 US dollars on advertising campaigns. That equates to over one million US dollars today, still a fraction of what today's companies spend at nearly 500 billion pounds globally.

E In this era, though, the medium with the greatest prevalence was oral. Public criers would circulate messages in urban centres to passers-by advertising various products. There is evidence of written adverts and for more than just selling wares. In one such advert found at the ruins of Thebes dated 1,000 BC, a man was offering a reward for a runaway slave. But oral messages were the main method of delivery until the invention of the printing press in 1450.

F But there was a time when an advert was a rare occurrence and its effect on society amounted to no more than its core function; that is, to connect seller and buyer. We know that the written word began around 5,000 years ago in Mesopotamia, in the Sumerian civilisation that existed in modern-day southern Iraq. The make-up of this early scrawling consisted of grain inventories, from what historians and linguists can make of it.

G Adverts in ancient times did contain an element of sophistication which essentially lured buyers, albeit less obviously. On the other side of the world, in ancient China, the language of adverts contained selling points and friendly imagery, such as in an advert to coax people into using a craftsman's services. This particular advertising medium is considered the oldest example of printed advertising.

H That formula was soon copied by other publishers looking to increase their profits while expanding their circulation. British newspapers, which had been using newspaper advertising since the 18th century, used adverts to promote books and the newspapers themselves. The printing press had made their production much more affordable and advertising content expanded to include medicines, in what would prove to be the first instances of false advertising.

Vocabulary

A Choose the correct option.

1 The programmes with the highest ratings are broadcast during _____ time.
   a chief   **b** prime   **c** key

2 I can't read the _____ under that photo – can you make out what it says?
   a caption   **b** subtitle   **c** legend

3 The advert has a catchy _____ that will make you tap your foot to it hours after hearing it.
   a clatter   **b** ringing   **c** jingle

4 The company poured millions into promotion at the _____ of product design.
   a detriment   **b** sacrifice   **c** expense

5 Most people don't look for jobs in a newspaper's _____ ads; they look online.
   a catalogued   **b** classified   **c** sorted

6 There are so many _____ on this motorway, it's a wonder no one has wrecked their vehicle.
   a billboards   **b** trailers   **c** panels

B Circle the odd one out. Then match it to the correct definition.

1	momentum	inertia	impetus	thrust	**a** a large book in a series
2	contradictory	hypocritical	insincere	frank	**b** give support to
3	forfeiture	purchase	acquisition	attainment	**c** a regular order, e.g. monthly
4	edition	publication	subscription	issue	**d** a loss from not participating
5	endorse	slander	defame	malign	**e** honest, forthright
6	column	volume	editorial	feature	**f** lack of movement

C Cross out the word that is incorrect.

1   If a company touts / tempts / pitches its product as the best in the world, it's probably not.
2   The mattress factory put out a half-price sale sign to try to coax / lure / sway people into the warehouse.
3   Film studios lobby / hype / talk up a bad film simply to trick people into seeing it.
4   Billing major celebrities in productions doesn't always amount / translate / account to big bucks at the box office.
5   I hardly ever read magazines; I usually just flick / toss / flip through them.
6   People often equate / liken / correlate material wealth with success.
7   High-end merchandise must have the degree / essence / feeling of luxury built into the brand.
8   Even though the house was falling apart, the buyers were sucked / drawn / pulled in by the estate agent's charm.

D Complete the sentences with these words.

driven   geared   get   push   rule   talk   wear   win

1   The product line may have to be discontinued altogether; we can't _____ out that option.
2   Let's ensure the marketing focus is _____ to the massive bank holiday sales weekend. I want all sales assistants on the floor.
3   You're not going to _____ anyone over by promoting the details of the service; try to get people to connect with it emotionally.
4   Telemarketers call repeatedly because they hope to _____ you down and make you buy something just to get them to go away.
5   The salesman uses subtle tactics; he knows that if you _____ people too hard into buying things, you can scare them off.
6   I can hardly _____ behind a product that's failed numerous safety inspections.
7   The greedy shoppers were _____ by unscrupulous sales rhetoric.
8   I loved the way this furniture looked the moment I saw it; you don't have to _____ me into buying it.

E Read the *Exam Reminder* and complete the *Exam Task*.

Exam Reminder

Coping with unknown words
- Have a look at all the answer choices for a gap and note those whose meaning you are unsure of.
- For those whose meaning you do know, try them in the gap to see if they work.
- If the words you know are not right, try each unknown word to see if they are possible.

Exam Task

For questions **1 – 8**, read the text below and decide which answer (**a**, **b**, **c** or **d**) best fits each gap.

It's all in the story

Companies use a variety of tactics to (1) _____ buyers into purchasing their products, a powerful one being the art of storytelling. Studies show that consumers across all (2) _____ connect with products not so much because of associated facts, features or specific attributes, but through emotions and personal feelings. Thus, hiring (3) _____ actors to tell a moving story about how a product has changed their lives or made the world a better place (4) _____ more people than saying the product works twice as well as the next brand or that it's made through a state-of-the-art manufacturing process. Such facts and figures can serve as strong (5) _____ of a product; however, (6) _____ an emotional response influences consumers threefold over mere content as regards television commercials and twofold in print ads. Thus, companies are willing to (7) _____ out on poignant, story-driven advertisements because of how (8) _____ they are of consumers.

1   a   endorse   b   hype   c   lobby   d   entice
2   a   demographics   b   geographic   c   biographic   d   photographic
3   a   mysterious   b   magnetic   c   charismatic   d   baffling
4   a   courts   b   woos   c   flatters   d   pursues
5   a   testimonies   b   infomercials   c   advertisements   d   endorsements
6   a   deducing   b   inducing   c   convincing   d   tempting
7   a   smack   b   spray   c   slap   d   splash
8   a   manipulative   b   controlling   c   unscrupulous   d   protective

Grammar

Countable & uncountable nouns; Indefinite Pronouns; Reciprocal & reflexive pronouns; Articles

A Complete the sentences with the correct form of the word given.

1 paper

Did you see the _____ today? Tom's picture is plastered all over them!

Can you load some _____ into the printer? It's completely out.

2 room

Could you please move over a bit? I haven't got any _____.

The printing _____ were abuzz with the sound of whirling machinery.

3 jam

The traffic _____ that occur in New York on a daily basis are staggering.

I'd like a large dollop of _____ on my toast, please.

4 currency

There used to be several _____ in Europe, but now it's mostly the Euro.

We're low on _____ and will have to order more from the central bank.

5 ground

A president can't lie under oath; that's _____ for impeachment.

We're got several journalists on the _____ covering the breaking story.

6 height

An athlete's _____ is often a factor in how well they play certain sports.

Sarah's award-winning reporting style allowed her to reach new _____ in her career.

B Circle the correct words.

1 Sadly, while all of these products look fantastic, any / none / some of them do what they say they will do.

2 I'm afraid I can't help you with the campaign; you'll have to ask someone other / – / else.

3 Much of this information is factual and informative, but few / little / some will appeal on an emotional level.

4 Please place all sharp objects in the container if you have none / any / some.

5 As soon as everyone / someone / anyone is here, we'll start the presentation.

6 We can't use these posters. Each of them is / has / have some kind of error.

7 I've received two different design layouts, but none / neither / no one of them is satisfactory.

8 This pen you gave me doesn't work. Have you got other / one / another?

C Complete the sentences with these words or phrases.

> herself   one another   ourselves   themselves   yourself

1 The three friends vowed to help _____ out when in need.

2 If you don't believe what I'm telling you about Liz, you can ask her _____.

3 The children were old enough to dress _____, so John left them to it.

4 There's nothing wrong with this campaign. The boss _____ approved it.

5 We don't need help selecting clothes. We can choose for _____.

D Circle the correct words.

1 A / The famous man once said that the / – adverts are the / – cave art of a / the modern era.

2 Always the / an itinerant saleswoman, Sofia has done business in the / – Netherlands, – / the UK and – / the France.

3 They say that – / an advertising has the / a way of turning a / the small thing into – / a really big thing.

4 A / The politician aimed his message not at the / – middle class or – / the poor, but a / the wealthy business class of his country.

5 A / One way to deal with the / an angry customer is to kill them with – / the kindness because, as they say, the / a customer is always right.

6 The / A famous author Mark Twain noted that many a / – small thing has been made a / – large by a / the right kind of advertising.

E Read the *Exam Reminder* and complete the *Exam Task*.

Exam Reminder

Thinking about determiners
- For gaps that require determiners, look at the surrounding text to decide if you need an article, pronoun or other type of determiner.
- Make sure the determiner matches the noun, if any, that it accompanies as regards the number and whether it is countable or uncountable.

Exam Task

For questions **1 – 8**, read the text below and think of the word which best fits each space. Use only **one** word in each space.

This page cannot be displayed

Surfing the web can be a cumbersome process. For **(1)** _____ who has had trouble loading a web page, it's often due to the insane amount of advertising embedded in the pages. It's an annoyance that many of us just have to put up with; we click on some semi-interesting link hoping the page will load straight away, only to be met with disappointment when we realise it's going to be one of **(2)** _____ pages that never, ever loads. We drum our fingers on our table or desk, telling **(3)** _____ that the page will appear any second now, only to give up in despair, close the browser and start again, if we can bear to.

The problem lies in the fact that web design is done with the assumption that **(4)** _____ viewing the web page is using a computer or mobile phone with **(5)** _____ swiftest of processors and which is connected to the internet through **(6)** _____ high-speed broadband connection. Also, websites work very hard to make sure you're bombarded with advertisements in hopes that you might buy **(7)** _____. But web designers and new sites need to face facts; if people's online experiences continue to deteriorate, the future of online advertising might very well be going **(8)** _____.

Listening

A Read the *Exam Reminder*. In Task 2 of the *Exam Task*, what kind of opinions – positive or negative – would you expect to hear given each choice, A–H?

_____

Exam Reminder

Focusing on attitude & opinion
- Listening to how speakers talk about a topic helps you to work out how they feel. Recognising their emotions can help you answer questions correctly.
- Naturally, it is important to listen to the speaker's words and expressions, but considering their intonation also gives clues to their attitudes and opinions.

B 10.1 ▶‖ Listen and complete the *Exam Task*.

Exam Task

You will hear five short extracts in which different people talk about buying new products.

Task 1

For questions **1 – 5**, choose from the list (**A – H**) the reason each person gives for buying new things.

Task 2

For questions **6 – 10**, choose from the list (**A – H**) what opinion each person expresses about advertising.

You will hear the recording twice. While you listen, you must complete both tasks.

Task 1	Task 2
A cajoled by another person	A influential for consumers
B keeping up with others	B confused by messaging
C the convenience of buying it	C pervasively bothersome
D a fantastic deal on offer	D dazzling to look at
E the pleasure of buying	E completely useless
F convinced by a free offer	F difficult to trust
G celebrity endorsements	G informative
H the necessity of the situation	H drives up product costs
1 Speaker 1 ☐	6 Speaker 1 ☐
2 Speaker 2 ☐	7 Speaker 2 ☐
3 Speaker 3 ☐	8 Speaker 3 ☐
4 Speaker 4 ☐	9 Speaker 4 ☐
5 Speaker 5 ☐	10 Speaker 5 ☐

C 10.2 ▶‖ Listen again and check your answers.

Writing: an article (3)

A Tick the topics that could include an element of narrative.

1 An international magazine has asked readers to send in articles giving their views on credit card debt. _____

2 You are going to write about the advantages and disadvantages of businesses using word-of-mouth advertising. _____

3 A magazine is looking to publish a story about how consumerism affects people in your community. _____

4 You are going to write about how companies approach advertising in developed countries versus developing countries. _____

5 You decide to submit an article about a friend who has a problem with brand addiction. _____

B Some of the partial narratives match topics from exercise A. Match a narrative to a topic, if possible, and put a cross for the ones that you would not use. Why are the ones you would not use inappropriate?

1 My colleague Jessica believes that when people talk about how terrific a product is, that goes much farther in promoting it than any television commercial, billboard or celebrity endorsement ever could. She claims that whenever a product impresses her – or conversely, lets her down – she tells all her friends, who tell all their friends and this domino effect is incredibly powerful. ☐

2 I think advertising affects behaviour in a rather negative way, if I think about how I often only purchase the most well-known brands. Take a look at my kitchen and products in which the manufacturers poured a great deal of resources into their advertising campaigns feature heavily on my shelves. You'll be hard-pressed to find a lesser-known brand anywhere in my house. ☐

3 My friend Justin's problem epitomises this out-of-control behaviour and I give you the following situation as an example. We are at a gathering with a mix of good friends and casual acquaintances. I overhear him talking to someone about their clothing label and saying, 'Oh, I don't buy that label. I find the quality isn't to my liking.' ☐

4 Take Meagan, for example. She and I have been friends all of our lives. When she started university, she was very against splashing out on clothing or other extraneous expenses. But at some point, she started using credit cards, and it soon snowballed out of control. I have never seen her as stressed as she was during that time. ☐

C Read these paragraphs and tick (✓) the ones that reference a previously mentioned character.

1 I would also like to point out that being addicted to certain brands equates to an unwillingness to try new things. Kevin's addiction means he lacks interest in considering anything outside of his established catalogue of luxury brands. Aside from being expensive, this habit robs an individual of variety, which is the spice of life, as they say. ☐

2 In addition to leading to out-of-control spending habits, it can truly be financially ruinous when it comes to paying bills which have reached figures that even the well-off would gasp at. It can force an individual into bankruptcy, which would then result in years of abysmal credit ratings that can put getting a mortgage out of reach. ☐

3 I would also like to point out that consumerism can cause the 'keeping up with the Joneses' effect. As I previously mentioned, I knew from my conversation with my neighbour that purchasing a luxury car was beyond their budget. It was not long after they got their new car that my other neighbour expressed a wish to trade in hers. ☐

D Read and complete the *Exam Task below*. Don't forget to use the *Useful Expressions* on page 151 of your Student's Book.

Exam Task

A magazine is looking for articles on brand addiction. You decide to submit an article about a friend of yours with this problem. Make comments on these points, giving your own point of view:
- Narrow-minded character
- Getting stuck in your ways
- Advice on breaking the habit

Write your **article** in 280–320 words.

↪ Writing Reference p. 207 in Student's Book

Vocabulary

A Choose the correct answers.

1 John's hard-working when supervised; left to his own _____, he becomes lazy.

   a means   **b** instruments

   c tools   **d** devices

2 They sped up the production process at the _____ of quality.

   a cost   **b** liability

   c expense   **d** payment

3 Sharon asked her former boss to provide her with a _____ to give to potential employers.

   a suggestion   **b** testimonial

   c reference   **d** memorandum

4 I doubt anyone will lose their job from the merger, but I can't _____ it out.

   a rule   **b** point

   c drive   **d** hear

5 The voting registration campaign was meant to _____ young people to register.

   a entice   **b** trigger

   c induce   **d** convert

6 I'm so depressed – I got served a(n) _____ notice today and have two weeks to find a new place.

   a repossession **b** dismissal

   c foreclosure   **d** eviction

7 I've been working so much lately that I'm in serious need of some _____.

   a overtime   **b** part-time

   c downtime   **d** full-time

8 I'm not trying to _____ you with too much work, but these 16 files need reviewing by Wednesday.

   a harness   **b** saddle

   c strap   **d** buckle

9 Sceptical of his colleague's motives, there was a certain _____ of cynicism in Mark's voice.

   a grade   **b** mark

   c degree   **d** unit

10 Kevin won't be back until next week – he's still on sick _____.

   a exit   **b** departure

   c leave   **d** consent

11 Can you give Nathan a hand? He's fallen _____ on his project.

   a through   **b** back

   c apart   **d** behind

12 Advertising campaigns with negative messages, like it or not, have the ability to _____ an election.

   a wave   **b** sway

   c rock   **d** bend

13 Robbie breathed a sigh of relief, as he was spared being given his marching _____ at his firm.

   a commands   **b** instructions

   c papers   **d** orders

14 Ms Leighton is away on a business trip, so I'll be conducting the meeting in her _____.

   a presence   **b** absence

   c essence   **d** existence

15 The laws of Spain don't apply in Portugal, as Portugal is a _____ nation.

   a liberated   **b** sovereign

   c neutral   **d** dependent

16 The company gives you a week's worth of training; after that, you have to _____ for yourself.

   a fend   **b** stand

   c cope   **d** hold

17 Television advertisements are the most effective way to improve market _____.

   a bit   **b** piece

   c share   **d** part

18 The economic recovery has lost some _____, as can be learnt from negative jobs reports.

   a momentum   **b** drive

   c thrust   **d** motion

19 His last work of art was superb, but I'm afraid his most recent piece is just _____.

   a generic   **b** mediocre

   c obligatory   **d** superficial

20 She hasn't given her support yet, but don't worry – I can talk her _____ it.

   a into   **b** out of

   c over   **d** through

Grammar

B **Choose the correct answers.**

1 I've sent you all the documents, but let me know if I left _____ out.
   a everything   **b** nothing
   c anything   **d** anyone

2 They hung a _____ posters round town to advertise the concert.
   a several   **b** deal of
   c number of   **d** great deal

3 I can't accept this bribe – it's unacceptable to conduct _____ this way.
   a business   **b** a business
   c the businesses   **d** businesses

4 Tom visited a landmark in the city centre and a park on the outskirts, and _____ were worth the trip.
   a both   **b** some
   c many   **d** each

5 The supervisor, many of _____ subordinates disliked him, was eventually relieved of his duties.
   a whom   **b** those
   c whose   **d** their

6 I have always wondered what different _____ circulated in the ancient world or if a bartering system was more commonly used.
   a currency   **b** currencies
   c money   **d** monies

7 Careful consideration was put into the ad campaign _____ offend anyone.
   a in order to   **b** so as to
   c supposing that   **d** so as not to

8 Let me give you _____ advice – read all of the label on the back before you buy a product.
   a a piece   **b** a piece of
   c piece of   **d** piece

9 As the saying goes, _____ bird in the hand is worth two in the bush.
   a –   **b** a
   c the   **d** any

10 I'm impressed with the new product line, but _____ the cost, we have to make some changes.
    a instead of   **b** much as
    c not that   **d** in view of

11 I know of an abandoned house on that street, but _____ house you're referring to has occupants.
    a –   **b** a
    c the   **d** one

12 Steven, _____ picked to lead the project, was warmly welcomed by his colleagues.
    a having   **b** having been
    c being   **d** was

13 The marketing manager and the production manager view _____ as rivals.
    a yourselves   **b** another
    c themselves   **d** each other

14 Henry, Beth and Lisa are highly skilled, but _____ of them know the business as well as Johanna.
    a any   **b** neither
    c none   **d** some

15 Out of these dozen or so ad designs, I only want you to select _____ very best.
    a those   **b** a
    c –   **d** the

16 Companies do many things to improve product sales and _____ particularly effective tactic is to advertise just before a holiday.
    a the   **b** no
    c one   **d** any

17 I don't have the authority to convince the board of these changes; you will have to do it _____.
    a myself   **b** ourselves
    c themselves   **d** yourself

18 I've tried many different household cleaners, and none _____ better than a mix of bleach and water.
    a are   **b** be
    c am   **d** is being

19 We can't force all of this information into one advert; _____ person can only absorb so much.
    a –   **b** a
    c the   **d** any

20 It can take hours to settle on a new computer, _____ such a wide variety of choices, each with its own features.
    a however   **b** much as
    c what with   **d** not that

Use of English

C Read the text below and decide which answer (a, b, c or d) best fits each gap.

The fulfilling gap year

Gap years are quite common in many parts of the world and most young people, upon leaving high school, feel (**1**) _____ to one. It's plain to see how the idea would be (**2**) _____; taking a year off from studies to travel the world and consider your future sounds like bliss. Adverts for gap years contain (**3**) _____ that read 'The best year of my life' and 'Total adventure, Totally rewarding', and offer the newly (**4**) _____ student the opportunity to learn more about themselves while learning about the world.

Of course, a gap year shouldn't be (**5**) _____ as just a time to party, and as attractive as it may sound, one must not get (**6**) _____ in by that notion. One way to make the most of this time is to get involved in some inspiring voluntary work abroad. There is more than a (**7**) _____ of truth in the idea that immersion in a new culture will teach you more about yourself than any classroom ever would. It will allow you to reach a level of emotional (**8**) _____ that will stay with you for a lifetime.

1 a permitted	**b** entitled	**c** designated	**d** allowed
2 a teasing	**b** touting	**c** tempting	**d** taunting
3 a captions	**b** billboards	**c** jingles	**d** editions
4 a emancipated	**b** liberated	**c** independent	**d** sovereign
5 a dismissed	**b** denied	**c** denounced	**d** dissuaded
6 a pulled	**b** sucked	**c** forced	**d** swept
7 a mark	**b** grade	**c** degree	**d** notch
8 a wisdom	**b** ripeness	**c** adulthood	**d** maturity

D Complete the sentences with the correct form of the words in bold.

Creative job security

One of the best ways to avoid a (**1**) _____ from work is to make yourself (**2**) _____ around the office. If a company ever decides to lay people off, managers often make emotional decisions. As such, hard-working yet (**3**) _____ individuals might be more likely to get the sack over those who are lazy but have a more charming personality overall.

So how does one secure a position high up in the (**4**) _____ structure? Some good advice is to generate a buzz about yourself. Talking to everyone in the company, from the post room assistant to the CEO, can result in the (**5**) _____ of valuable knowledge about specific processes in the organisation. Then, making the higher-ups believe you're the only one who knows it – without seeming (**6**) _____, of course – might just shield you from a job loss. It takes months of the right moves to accomplish this, though, but if you genuinely like the company you work for and are not doing it just to save your job, then there's nothing (**7**) _____ about building this kind of rapport with your superiors. If and when that fateful day comes, they might feel they have a(n) (**8**) _____ to keep you on board, lest the company will suffer without the integral cog that is you.

DISMISS

DISPENSE

CHARISMA

HIERARCHY

ACQUIRE

MANIPULATE

HYPOCRITE

OBLIGATE

E Complete the text with one word in each gap.

Consumerism in Greenland

Storytelling was once (**1**) _____ rich tradition in Greenland, but sadly, it's being killed off by consumerism. Whereas Greenlanders once used to gather round fires and tell stories to (**2**) _____ other, nowadays they sit in front of (**3**) _____ television watching Danish cartoons and American films. (**4**) _____ of these is subtitled in the local language, as Greenlander words are too long to fit on the screen. As a result, their linguistic heritage is threatened. And (**5**) _____ with the lifestyle and behaviour portrayed in mainstream films, Greenlanders are in danger of being sucked (**6**) _____ by a decadent lifestyle and wishing they (**7**) _____ were leading these kinds of lives.

All of this has allowed a kind of extreme loneliness to take hold. Thankfully, in (**8**) _____ to preserve their rich stories as well as their language, a linguist from the UK, Stephen Pax Leonard, has chosen to station (**9**) _____ in the region. He transcribes local languages (**10**) _____ that they will live on for posterity, giving Greenlanders hope that their heritage will not be forgotten.

F Complete the second sentence so that it has a similar meaning to the first sentence, using the word given. Do not change the word given. You must use between three and eight words, including the word given.

1 Paul checked Tim's work, while Tim checked Ryan's and Ryan checked Paul's.

one

Paul, Tim and Ryan _____ work.

2 They gave the project to a new carpenter and his craftsmanship was shoddy.

whom

The new carpenter _____ shoddy craftsman.

3 Well-informed consumers won't be fooled by this campaign.

winning

The campaign will not succeed at _____ well-informed.

4 So that she wouldn't get burnt by the sun, she bought a large hat.

as

She bought a large hat _____ the sun.

5 Many products were damaged by the time they arrived.

deal

A _____ upon arrival.

6 He was fired from the company because he performed poorly.

view

In _____ off from the company.

Reading

A Read the *Exam Reminder*. Which questions in the *Exam Task*, including in any answer options, directly ask you to consider the author's viewpoint?

_____

B Now complete the *Exam Task*.

Too young to be famous?

The machine that is celebrity culture has given us the meteoric rise and fall of the child actor, with plenty of cautionary tales to point to and ask if something should have been done to prevent them. Recently, the Chinese government took the extreme and unprecedented measure of banning the children of celebrities from appearing in any type of reality TV programming, in an effort to prevent the manufacturing of child stars. It would appear that perhaps limiting the exposure a child has to fame serves to protect and ensure a solid, stable upbringing.

The pressure of fame is undoubtedly onerous, even for adults, who, despite growing up out of the spotlight, sometimes buckle under the stress of stardom they achieved later in life and exhibit all manner of behavioural disorders after their stardom has waned. The same can be said of child actors, but the effect is seemingly multiplied by the fact that, if achieving stardom as children, their view of reality is possibly warped and they may never even have the chance to acquire the necessary coping skills. But given that some child actors – in fact, most – can make a go of their careers into adulthood, are children really so incapable of handling such pressure or is there actually no problem at all?

Banning children from acting has an element of common sense to it, but imagine, if you will, television programmes, films and so forth absent of children. As this sort of media is supposed to reflect real life, it would seem surreal if there were no children in these stories, as if children had ceased to exist altogether. While the Chinese government's move to limit the exposure of children may seem well intentioned, at least on the surface, it is not entirely realistic to say that children are not allowed to appear on the small or big screen. Of course, they are applying it to one particular media – that of reality TV; nonetheless, is such a ban sensible for any type of media?

Upon closer examination of the phenomenon of the child star, we see examples both of success and failure. How many of each do we have? Is there a disproportionately high amount of failure in the lives of child actors if we look at the statistics and compare their problems with those of ordinary people? We see a child star fail and we immediately blame fame, but what about the success stories of other child actors such as Jodie Foster, Daniel Radcliffe and Leonardo DiCaprio, all of whom got their start as very young children? Are we to credit fame for their success in the same way we blame it for others' failures?

In the case of the latter, these are the stars we know about, as they went on to achieve long-lasting fame, even top acting awards. Child stars are not always destined to eternally seek the limelight, however, so there are many cases of success stories that people often don't know about. Peter Ostrum, who played Charlie Bucket in *Willy Wonka & the Chocolate Factory*, went on to pursue a doctorate in veterinary medicine. Shirley Temple, leading box-office star in the 1930s from the age of seven, became a politician and the first female US ambassador. Polish child stars and identical twin brothers Lech and Jarosław Kaczynski gave up acting and were respectively elected as president and prime minister of Poland, positions they held at the same time.

Invariably, though, it's the catastrophic demise that we hear about, not just of child actors, of course, but when it does happen to them, we feel a mixture of sorrow and disbelief. To date, there is little statistical evidence to support the claim that fame and celebrity culture ruin the lives of child actors; the only proof we have is what we perceive to be true. Protections are in place, to an extent, to help ensure that children have as normal an upbringing as possible. California, for example, has enacted laws which mandate that children must continue with their educational studies exactly as they would if they weren't in films, even going so far as to require teachers on set if need be. In this vein, ensuring support for child actors may need to go further than the broad restrictions exercised by China.

You are going to read an article about the phenomenon of child stars. For questions **1 – 6**, choose the answer (**a, b, c** or **d**) which you think fits best according to the text.

1   What can be said about the measure taken by the Chinese as regards child stars?
   a   It is a view fully endorsed by the author.
   b   It will prevent the phenomenon of child stars.
   c   It will prohibit children from acting in films.
   d   It's something they've never done before.

2   In the second paragraph, the author implies that children
   a   are better equipped to handle fame than adults.
   b   never learn coping skills when they are famous young.
   c   may or may not suffer harmful effects of fame.
   d   are destined to be abnormal adults if they are famous young.

3   How does the author view the government ban in the third paragraph?
   a   He is not certain it was born of good intentions.
   b   He agrees with the implementation of the ban.
   c   He thinks it is useless in the case of reality TV.
   d   He believes the intention is to control the media.

4   In the fourth paragraph, the author suggests that
   a   fame is to blame for the problems of child stars.
   b   fame is unlikely to have a role in the failure of a star.
   c   the fame of some stars shows it has no harmful effect.
   d   the failure of certain stars means that fame is harmful.

5   The author presents the examples in the fifth paragraph to demonstrate that
   a   child actors are capable of achieving anything they want.
   b   fame can repel some from a long acting career.
   c   a more exhaustive study of the subject is necessary to evaluate it.
   d   success can open the door to other positions in life.

6   The author concludes by saying that
   a   nothing can protect a child from the dangers of fame.
   b   taking measures to help children cope with fame is worth considering.
   c   our belief in the dangers of fame is greater than the reality.
   d   children should be educated in how to deal with fame.

Vocabulary

A   Circle the correct words.

1   Her memoirs / excerpts cover her life from when she entered politics until when she became president.
2   Forcing me to give you £100,000 to keep quiet about my criminal past amounts to slander / blackmail.
3   After the dictator was removed from power, he was forced to live in obscurity / exile on a remote deserted island.
4   I'm afraid he's not going to be a credible / feasible witness for your case, as his story has a number of holes in it.
5   After a string / splash of flops at the cinema, his career was all but finished.
6   Aladdin, the eminent / fabled character of a story set in the Middle East, was actually from China.
7   The actor was stalked / hounded by reporters the moment he stepped out of his house.
8   She's only had six months in the stardom / limelight; how can she already think she's a legend?
9   Jill has been writing a(n) anecdote / column for The Times for 15 years now.
10   In carving statues of themselves, Roman emperors looked to become immortal / illustrious, as their likeness would live on for eternity.

B   Complete the sentences with the words not used in exercise A.

1   The actress was being _____ by a strange man over the course of two months, so she filed a restraining order against him.
2   If you make untrue accusations about me, I'll be suing you for _____!
3   Few actors who achieve _____ are happy with everything it has to offer.
4   While we were waiting for the curtain to go up, our guest told us a funny _____ about a time he was mistaken for a famous actor and had to flee from fans.
5   Thomas's protégé made a big _____ on the opening night of the production.
6   She was quite popular on television in the 1990s, but since then, she has more or less faded into _____.
7   Thousands turned out to mourn the death of their beloved, _____ king.
8   The author read a few _____ from his new crime novel that was about to be published.
9   The _____ astronomer announced the discovery of water on the large asteroid.
10   While it is _____ to fool the press for a period of time, you can't fool them forever.

C Choose the correct answers.

1 Whoever _____ this story to the press is going to be in serious trouble.
   a seeped   b dropped   c dripped   d leaked

2 I can let you in on some details, but please be _____; I don't want the whole world knowing.
   a discreet   b reserved   c distant   d aloof

3 Rummaging through a film star's rubbish is the ultimate _____ of privacy.
   a conquest   b invasion   c assault   d blitz

4 When the press started contacting her relatives, she knew things were getting _____ hand.
   a in   b out of   c into   d away from

5 After three years of poor performances, the singer was finally on the verge of making a _____.
   a renewal   b comeback   c rebirth   d awakening

6 The scandal meant that the tennis player was _____ from many sponsorship deals.
   a dropped   b cancelled   c fired   d disposed

D Complete the sentences with one word in each gap.

1 Upwards _____ 30,000 spectators turned out to hear the politician's speech.

2 When the famous actor parachuted onto the crowd, amazed as they were, they knew it was _____ the top.

3 It took Nigel six years before he finally got signed _____ a major record label.

4 He was so impressed with Lisa's audition that he hired her _____ the spot.

5 No one understood the director's reasoning in praising a dictator; unfortunately, the remark just seemed _____ very bad taste.

6 His complete lack of talent as a director was _____ odds with his immense talent as an actor.

7 By the time she was 19, she had reached the peak _____ her success and it was all downhill from there.

8 There's no end to the kind of stunts people will pull _____ the name of fame.

E Read the *Exam Reminder* and complete the *Exam Task*.

Exam Reminder

Creating prefixes & suffixes from the same word
- You might have to add two or even three affixes to a word, as many will require both a prefix and one or two suffixes, e.g. *surprise* → *unsurprisingly*.
- Look at the words surrounding the gap to determine what part of speech is needed.
- A prefix will be required for negative words and in some cases a positive word, e.g. *cover* → *recoverable*, and you will use suffixes to form a part of speech.

Exam Task

For questions **1 – 8**, read the text below. Use the word given in capitals at the end of some of the lines to form a word that fits in the space in the same line.

Missing: world's most famous mystery writer

When it comes to mystery writers, **(1)** _____ novelist Agatha Christie did more than just put   **CLAIM**
stories to paper – she was once part of a mystery herself. In December 1926, the writer **(2)** _____   **NOTORIETY**
went missing for 11 days, setting off a frantic search. Her disappearance made **(3)** _____   **NATION**
news headlines, including on the front page of the *New York Times*.

Foreign **(4)** _____ descended on Sunningdale, England, the location of her home   **CORRESPOND**
and last sighting, to cover the dramatic event. Even fellow mystery writer, the **(5)** _____   **ILLUSTRATE**
Sir Arthur Conan Doyle, creator of Sherlock Homes, joined the search. Authorities quickly
found Agatha's car abandoned by the side of the road. After days of fruitless searches,
she was eventually spotted at an elegant spa resort in Harrogate, living under an assumed
identity – that of her husband's mistress.

During the affair, **(6)** _____ theorists churned out their own explanations as to what   **CONSPIRE**
had happened. Some believed she had been murdered by her unfaithful husband and
others chalked it up as being a cleverly-crafted **(7)** _____ stunt to promote a new book.   **PUBLIC**
But as Agatha's memory of events never recovered, we cannot know for sure what
transpired; thus, the story will likely retain its **(8)** _____ nature.   **FAME**

Grammar

Gerunds; Common idiomatic expressions with gerunds; Infinitives; Gerund or Infinitive?

A Complete the sentences with the correct form of these verbs.

> blog   broadcast   edit   post   print   publish   type   write

1 They managed _____ his book on time and it's now available for online purchase.
2 I can't stand _____ this manuscript; it's loaded with errors!
3 They finished _____ the 200-page document, although they nearly ran out of ink.
4 They were afraid _____ the documentary on television due to its controversial nature.
5 This data has to be entered into the spreadsheet by the end of the day, so you had better _____ fast.
6 Mark is really into _____ and he likes to upload pictures that go along with his entries.
7 I know you don't believe he's going to get fired, but I'm afraid the _____ is on the wall.
8 Blake got into trouble for _____ a nasty tweet about his ex-girlfriend.

B Circle the correct words.

1 Do you fancy to attend / attending / attend Mike's book signing with me?
2 I think I would rather reading / to read / read a true-crime novel than something purely fictional.
3 It's no use to ask / asking / ask him to sign autographs; he's quite full of himself now and won't do it.
4 You sent your letter to the publisher ages ago; do you expect hearing / to hear / hear from them soon?
5 We're planning to discuss / discussing / discuss storylines for the upcoming publication.
6 I can't believe they let him enter / to enter / entering the restaurant given what happened last time.
7 I wish the publisher could afford hire / hiring / to hire a professional photographer for the travel book.
8 The production crew spent a lot of time to build / build / building the elaborate set pieces.

C Complete the dialogues with the correct form of the verbs in brackets.

1 **A:** Why isn't Daniel working on his book?
   B: He stopped _____ (**do**) some research in the library.

2 **A:** I'm still upset about your harsh critique of Henry's work.
   B: I know. I do regret _____ (**say**) those things.

3 **A:** Where are Denise and Sonya?
   B: They stopped _____ (**pick**) up some supplies at a shop.

4 **A:** You've got to start putting more energy into your duties.
   B: Oh, would you please stop _____ (**nag**) me about it?!

5 **A:** John will be joining us at the theatre tonight.
   B: Ah, I remember _____ (**meet**) him last summer. What a lovely chap!

6 **A:** I can't seem to get this door open.
   B: Try _____ (**pull**) on the handle a little harder.

D Complete the idiomatic expressions with one word in each gap.

1 Kyle, don't be upset about the game. It's not the _____, but the taking part that counts.
2 His paintings are awful, but they sell for big bucks. I guess there's no _____ for bad taste.
3 I know it's a very prestigious institution, but send them an application anyway. There's no _____ in trying.
4 Congratulations on your new job! Here's _____ for a bright future!
5 This is a beautiful boat you've built, but let's see if it'll sail. After all, the proof of the pudding is in the _____.
6 I've changed this design layout a dozen times and the clients still don't like it. I guess there's no _____ some people.
7 Every week there's a new dramatic development in this story. There's just no _____ what will happen next.
8 Well, how about that … you've just got your driving licence. Here's _____ at you, kid!

E Read the *Exam Reminder* and complete the *Exam Task*.

Exam Reminder

Using a process of elimination

- You can eliminate an answer choice if it does not collocate, it does not fit grammatically or it has the wrong meaning for the sentence.
- If you can eliminate enough answer choices, you can choose the correct answer even if you are not sure of the meaning of the word you are choosing.

Exam Task

Read the passage, then select the word or phrase that fills the blank in both meaning and grammar.

Surely there's no harm in telling the truth!

US swimmer and Olympian Ryan Lochte landed in hot water for (**1**) _____ a robbery incident during the 2016 Rio Olympics. He said that he and three of his fellow athletes were held at gunpoint after an armed gang made their taxi (**2**) _____ in order to mug them. Brazilian police began investigating and discovered a videotape which told a different story. It seems that the swimmers had been out (**3**) _____ and stopped at a petrol station (**4**) _____ the toilet facilities. The video shows Lochte vandalising property, and the only people armed were security guards (**5**) _____ the grounds.

As these details emerged, the Brazilian authorities told the athletes that they were not allowed (**6**) _____ to their home countries, although Lochte was already back in the US at that point. Eventually, Lochte chose (**7**) _____ that he lied in order to salvage his image, but the damage was done. Several sponsors dropped him, and while Lochte's performance as a swimmer is remarkable, there's no (**8**) _____ for bad behaviour, especially from an Olympian.

	a	b	c	d
1	to fabricating	to fabricate	fabricating	fabricate
2	stopping	stop	to stop	to stopping
3	club	clubbing	to club	to clubbing
4	to using	using	use	to use
5	to patrolling	patrolling	patrol	to patrol
6	to return	return	to leave	leave
7	admitting	to admit	to admitting	admit
8	excuse	knowing	pleasing	hoping

Listening

A Read the *Exam Reminder*. Which questions in the *Exam Task* ask you to listen for opinions?

_____

B 🔊 **11.1** Listen and complete the *Exam Task*.

Exam Reminder

Listening between the lines

- Speakers often express their opinions indirectly; thus, the correct answer is often implied, not stated.
- Leave answers you do not know for the second listening so that you can answer other, perhaps easier, questions.

Exam Task

You will hear part of a discussion between Marty, a fashion photographer, and Lauren, a talent agent, about the paparazzi's role in society. For questions **1 – 5**, choose the answer (**a**, **b**, **c** or **d**) which fits best according to what you hear.

1 How could Lauren's 'true feelings' about the paparazzi be summarised?
  a They are unfairly blamed for mishaps.
  b Their negative characteristics keep them from ever being a positive force.
  c They have a rather valuable role in the publishing industry.
  d Their impact is overly emphasised.

2 What do Marty and Lauren agree on about the quality of the paparazzi's work?
  a The subject matter of the photos is often of importance.
  b There are some rare photos that are worthy of being viewed.
  c The technical skills are admirable.
  d The messy, unintentional style is never a desirable quality.

3 Lauren compares the paparazzi to professional photographers by
  a saying the result of their work is often very similar.
  b asserting they both have their own dark sides to contend with.
  c implying the value of their work is on an equal footing.
  d saying one tries to emulate the other's images, in essence.

4 What is Lauren's attitude regarding the paparazzi's skills?
  a She's in awe of their skills, as she knows from her own training how difficult getting a good shot is.
  b She admires their skill, even though it's rooted in dishonesty.
  c She doesn't admire their work because they lack formal training.
  d She thinks they're skilful and says it's due to on-the-job training.

5 Regarding placing restrictions on the paparazzi, Marty states that he
  a does not condone any physically imposed limitations.
  b is thankful that they cannot act without limits.
  c believes this is unfair, as their work has inspired him.
  d wishes there were a special task force to tackle to issue.

11 Say Cheese!

C 🔊 **11.2** Listen again and check your answers.

Writing: a review (2)

A Use these adjectives and nouns to form phrases. Then match the phrases to the appropriate type of review. Some adjectives may match more than one noun, and some phrases may be appropriate for more than one type of review.

captivating clichéd
commanding convoluted
disappointing electrifying
gripping harmonious
intended main poignant
romantic sweeping
underlying

anecdotes audience
cinematography direction
documentary melodies
performance plot presence
protagonist sound storyline
theme tragedy

Learning Reminder

Understanding the purpose of a review

- Remember to write a review containing information that you yourself would want to learn about a place, book, film, etc.
- Use vocabulary that fits what you are reviewing and, after finishing the informative part of the review, write a recommendation. This is the ultimate purpose of your review.
- Make sure your opinions and recommendation match.

Film review	Book review	Concert review

B Complete the sentences from various reviews with phrases from exercise A.

1 The star of the _____ is a master sushi chef and a total perfectionist.

2 All of us concert goers were energised by the _____ coming from the guitar player's riffs as he glided across the stage.

3 While the novel's _____ is adolescents looking for fantasy and escapism, people of all ages can find something to enjoy from this title.

4 What the film offers is a _____ about a man who constantly struggles to please his customers.

5 Set in a dystopian future, the _____ of the story is Winston Smith and he is tasked with rewriting history so that it supports the government that employs him.

C Read the partial sections of a review of a documentary on the art of sushi making. In which part of the plan on page 167 of your Student's Book would you put them?

1 I enjoyed seeing Jiro be deeply observant of his patrons and utterly dedicated to his craft. _____

2 Seldom do you see a style of film dedicated to a cooking technique. This is what makes it worth watching. _____

3 It is by far and away the best 80 minutes you could ever watch about this culinary art form, even if you're not a fan of raw fish. _____

4 This compelled me to watch a documentary titled *Jiro Dreams of Sushi*, which chronicles the daily life of an 85-year-old sushi maker still in search of perfect sushi. _____

5 Jiro Ono is a master sushi chef and a complete perfectionist. His sushi bar is tucked away in the basement of a Tokyo high-rise building. _____

D Read and complete the *Exam Task* below. Don't forget to use the *Useful Expressions* on page 167 of your Student's Book.

Exam Task

You recently saw a documentary and have decided to write a review of it for your local newspaper. In your review, you should describe the documentary, say what you liked or disliked about it and explain why you feel or do not feel it is worth viewing.

Write your **review** in 280–320 words.

▶ Writing Reference p. 206 in Student's Book

Reading

A Read the *Exam Reminder*. Next to which parts of the text in the *Exam Task* would you write *1*?

_____

B Now complete the *Exam Task*.

A map of the heavens

A Our night sky has mesmerised humanity for millennia, and given mankind's desire to map the planet, it makes perfect sense that the heavens would be mapped as well. We can trace the first instances of constellations being recorded back to the ancient Babylonian civilisation of Mesopotamia, or present-day Iraq. There, archaeologists have uncovered stone and clay tablets inscribed in 3,000 BCE, and more recent ones display the groups upon which the stellar cartographers of ancient Greece based the classical stellar patterns with which we are familiar today. Their relevance in our modern world is essentially historical, as we now use navigational equipment to discern latitudinal and longitudinal positions. In the ancient world, however, the constellations served as beacons, directing ships and foot travellers alike to their destinations with efficiency.

B Officially, there are 88 modern constellations recognised by the International Astronomical Union, or IAU. Of those, 48 were defined by the Greco-Egyptian writer, astronomer and mathematician Claudius Ptolemy in his astronomical treatise, the multi-chaptered *Almagest*, in the 2nd century. Given Ptolemy resided in the Northern Hemisphere, his celestial coordinate system was limited to this region alone. This was also true for the Babylonians, the ancient Chinese and the Arabs, all of whom catalogued their own stellar patterns but were equatorially situated to the north. For that reason, constellations of the Southern Hemisphere were not identified until several centuries later; in the 1500s to 1800s. Dutch navigators Pieter Dirkszoon Keyser and Frederick de Houtman were the first to designate new ones. More were to come, but not all were accepted; for example, Quadrans Muralis, created by French astronomer Jerome Lalande, never took hold, but to this day the Quadrantid meteor shower retains the obsolete constellation's name.

C The names of constellations arose more from symbolism rather than their actual appearance and as constellations fell under different naming systems in different civilisations, their names reveal characteristics of who made them. One of the most recognisable constellations is known as the Plough in the UK because to the inhabitants of this region, it looked like a plough, which can be vaguely seen in how the bottom grouping of stars looks like the device used to till soil and the top grouping looks like the part that is used to push it. In the US, it is known as the Big Dipper, as to people there, it seemed more like a ladle. To the Mayas, it was called a parrot and the Egyptians saw it as the limbs of a bull. The ancient Romans called it Ursae Majoris, or Greater Bear, a version of which, Ursa Major, serves as the official name with the IAU.

D Chinese, Indian and Middle Eastern civilisations all crafted their own systems of constellations, which both influenced and were influenced by Western systems. Parallels between Babylonian and ancient Chinese catalogues demonstrate that their systems influenced each other's development. Akin to our Zodiacal constellations were the Twenty-Eight Mansions, a representation of Chinese astrology based on lunar movements, rather than the sun. Evidence of Indian astronomy originated in the Indus Valley Civilisation in the north-western Indian subcontinent, a civilisation which thrived in the 3rd millennium BCE. In contrast to these two civilisations, Islamic astronomy was developed during the Islamic Golden Age, an era that spanned from the 8th to 15th centuries. The Arabs crafted thousands of manuscripts devoted to astronomy and dozens of celestial bodies are still referred to by their Arabic names.

E That said, with the advent of navigational systems, the constellations are decidedly less relevant today, at least diurnally. In the field of astronomy, however, scientists habitually refer to them as place markers for new discoveries, such as an exoplanet, quasar, pulsar, black hole or other celestial body unknown up until now. Naturally, constellations could only be used to determine what part of the sky an astronomer would peer into to see the object. Our view of the constellations exists in a two-dimensional plane, but in galactic space, the group of stars in a single constellation are often hundreds of light-years away from one another. In fact, because all the objects of the night sky are in constant motion and are eternally moving away or towards one another, the constellations we have come to know and love today will, in tens to hundreds of thousands of years, be unrecognisable, scattering like cosmic mist across our vast universe.

You are going to read an extract from an encyclopaedia entry on constellations. For questions **1 – 10**, choose from the sections (**A – E**). The sections may be chosen more than once.

In which section are the following mentioned?

1 a unit of measurement designating a thousand years. ☐

2 a spectacular event in the night sky ☐

3 imaginary lines that mark the Earth ☐

4 a pattern of travel defined by the moon ☐

5 people whose job it is to make maps ☐

6 something characterised as being flat ☐

7 an instrument used in farming ☐

8 a smaller part of a very large piece of land ☐

9 a place name in the Middle East ☐

10 a single, very large piece of writing ☐

Vocabulary

A **Complete the sentences with these words.**

archives   artefacts   heirlooms   legacy
memorial   reign   revival   vestiges

1 The 19th-century _____ of Queen Victoria of England was marked by prosperity and great change.

2 All historical documents are kept in the _____ on the bottom floor of the building.

3 Tomorrow the _____ service commemorating the country's independence from foreign rule is taking place.

4 There has been a(n) _____ of early 20th-century art forms in architecture of late.

5 These ornate dishes are _____ that have been passed down in my family for generations.

6 When a incumbent president is about to step down from office, they often think about what _____ they will leave behind.

7 These dilapidated wooden shacks are the only _____ of the people who settled in this community.

8 While on holiday in the Middle East, Deborah and her husband stumbled across some 5th-century _____ near a deserted temple.

B **Complete the sentences with the correct form of one of the words in bold.**

1 The holidaymakers were forced to live _____ when they were stranded for six days in a cabin with no electricity. (**primitive / nature**)

2 Many _____ noted that the debate dialogue had taken on a darker tone than in past years. (**observe / offer**)

3 I don't mean any _____, but I'm afraid that this logo is a bit culturally insensitive. (**respect / condemn**)

4 A great _____ can speak for long periods of time and never lose the attention of the audience. (**oral / vocal**)

5 The native people successfully fought the government to reclaim their _____ lands. (**ancestry / descend**)

6 This documentary _____ the lives of Mongolian nomads moving from place to place through harsh winters. (**chronic / renew**)

7 I can't read what this inscription says, as the writing is quite _____. (**blur / haze**)

8 The two countries signed a historic peace treaty to _____ their relations. (**moral / norm**)

C Circle the correct words.

1 As the violent protestors came nearer, the police **closed / joined** ranks to fend them off.

2 To promote better **diversity / integration**, the government offered free language courses to the refugees.

3 I could tell by his **mannerisms / assumptions** that he was brought up very well.

4 When the Roman emperor Caligula made his horse a senator, people knew he had gone **insensitive / insane**.

5 The speaker is running a bit late, so **stay / sit** tight and hopefully we'll start very soon.

6 If the queen had met a punk rocker, one could imagine witnessing a major **battle / clash** of cultures.

7 The show was so **satirical / irreverent** that most of the audience left feeling offended.

8 The **defiance / dispute** couldn't be solved amicably, so the two parties took it to court.

D Complete the sentences with compound adjectives formed with two of these words.

aged deep ever full hearted held honoured length light middle old present
rooted strongly time time

1 I love the _____ cafes that line the streets of my home town, as they remind me of an era long since past.

2 The sneaky politician stirred up _____ fears in the public to garner votes.

3 My cousins have got some _____ beliefs that are often opposite from mine.

4 The historian was a _____ man who was very knowledgeable about the British monarchy.

5 They watched a _____ documentary on 1990s Seattle punk bands.

6 The values instilled in our constitution are still _____ today.

7 The children listened to their grandparents tell _____ stories about life in the 1950s.

8 It is a _____ tradition in some cultures that the father gives away his daughter at her wedding.

E Read the *Exam Reminder* and complete the *Exam Task*.

Exam Reminder

Predicting the answer

- To predict answers, first read the text quickly to get the general idea, then go back and look at the gaps and the words surrounding them to see if you can think of the answer before you look at the answer choices.

- After you have guessed as many as you can, look at the answer choices to see if your guesses are there. For the ones you have trouble with, cross out the answer choices you know are wrong and then decide between the remaining choices.

Exam Task

For questions **1 – 8**, read the text below and decide which answer (**a**, **b**, **c** or **d**) best fits each gap.

Matriarchal societies

There are a handful of cultures in the world in which women have a(n) (**1**) _____ tradition of holding the power in the family. The Minangkabau, a(n) (**2**) _____ tribe of inhabitants residing in West Sumatra, Indonesia, is the largest such tribe known today, at four million people. According to tribal (**3**) _____, property is passed from mother to daughter and, in general, the mother is considered the most prominent member of society. While clan leaders are male, women can remove them from their position if they do not (**4**) _____ to the community's rules.

Another such group is the Mosuo, who live near Tibet. They share similarities with the Minangkabau, in that girls (**5**) _____ the family's possessions and, furthermore, females play the leading role in the (**6**) _____ of marriage. They practise what is known as a 'walking marriage', in which the marriage (**7**) _____ amounts to a woman walking to the man's home, thereby establishing him as her spouse. In both societies, there is a separation of powers and people of both genders believe that this keeps them on an equal (**8**) _____.

1	a	old-world	b	long-standing	c	ever-present	d	long-gone
2	a	racial	b	folkloric	c	primitive	d	indigenous
3	a	law	b	act	c	norm	d	type
4	a	follow	b	adhere	c	obey	d	observe
5	a	inherit	b	receive	c	obtain	d	gather
6	a	procedure	b	routine	c	ritual	d	habit
7	a	performance	b	ceremony	c	observance	d	execution
8	a	position	b	stability	c	balance	d	footing

Grammar

Cleft sentences with *it*; Cleft sentences with *what* & *all*

A Use this sentence to complete the cleft sentences. Begin your sentences with *It*.

Baron Pierre de Coubertin, a French educator, helped start the modern Olympic Games in Athens in 1896 at the Panathenaic Stadium.

1 _____ that Baron Pierre de Coubertin helped start in Athens in 1896.

2 _____ called Baron Pierre de Coubertin that helped start the modern Olympic Games.

3 _____ at the Panathenaic Stadium where the modern Olympic Games began.

4 _____, a French educator, who helped start the modern Olympic Games in 1986.

5 _____ where the first modern Olympic Games took place in Athens in 1896.

B Rewrite the sentences as cleft sentences that emphasise the phrases in bold. Begin your sentences with *It*.

1 The national anthem of the UK was written by **an unknown composer**.

_____

2 The Phoenicians brought the olive tree to Spain **6,000 years ago**.

_____

3 Joan of Arc, a heroine of France, died **during battle** in Normandy in 1431.

_____

4 Peanut butter wasn't invented by **George Washington Carver**, but rather, the Incas.

_____

5 **A Viking** named Lief Erickson truly discovered America, according to some.

_____

C Rewrite the sentences as cleft sentences using the word given. More than one answer may be possible.

1 They eat only fruit, vegetables and simple grains for 40 days.
all

_____

2 We know that the excavation site was inhabited in 3,150 BC.
about

_____

3 The townsfolk finished celebrating Carnival after two weeks.
later

_____

4 As they performed the ritual, they wore ceremonial garb.
what

_____

5 The villagers decorated the town square and cleared the main street of cars.
did

_____

D Complete the blog entry with *what* or *all*.

---

4 July   Family feast

Every 4th of July my extended family comes to our house to celebrate Independence Day in the US. We take care of the cooking and decorating, and (1) _____ my grandparents, aunts, uncles and cousins have to do is show up! (2) _____ my sister and I do is hang the bunting around the house. My mom serves loads of food so (3) _____ she does the night before is she cooks most of it and refrigerates it, and then (4) _____ she has to do on the 4th is just warm it up. My dad and brother are in charge of seating arrangements, so (5) _____ they do is set the tables and chairs up outside. My dad also does a bit of cooking, although not really a whole lot. Basically, (6) _____ he does is grill meat! (7) _____ I really enjoy about the event is seeing those family members who I don't normally see because they live so far away. Luckily, we have video chat, so (8) _____ we have to do is go online to see each other, but still, nothing beats spending time together with a gorgeous meal in front of us!

E Read the *Exam Reminder* and complete the *Exam Task*.

Exam Task

For questions **1 – 5**, complete the second sentence so that it has a similar meaning to the first sentence, using the word given. **Do not change the word given.** You must use between **three** and **eight** words, including the word given.

1 The stupendous finale of fireworks gave spectators a fright.

   scared

   It _____
   the spectators so much.

2 A kettle heats up water for beverages and nothing more.

   does

   All _____
   water for beverages.

3 Jonas Salk developed a vaccine for polio in the 1950s.

   when

   It _____
   a vaccine for polio.

4 The invention needs just one more part to work.

   needed

   All _____
   is just one more part.

5 I would always tell the truth in an interview.

   never

   What _____
   lie.

Listening

A Read the *Exam Reminder*. Which words in the *Exam Task* questions and answer choices have negative meanings? Which question contains a double negative?

_____

B 🔊 **12.1** Listen and complete the *Exam Task*.

Exam Task

You will hear three short segments from a radio programme. The programme is called *Life and Times*. You will hear what three different radio guests have to say about three different topics. After each talk, you will be asked some questions. From the three answer choices given, you should choose the one that best answers the question according to the information you heard.

Segment One

1 What does Ravi do when he discusses the physics of the ritual?

   a dispels a myth about the danger

   b negates the value of the practice

   c emphasises the risks of the ritual

2 What happens to people's heart rates during the ritual?

   a It accelerates rapidly.

   b They all have the same rate.

   c It is the same as their breathing.

Segment Two

3 Members of the upper classes formed clubs

   a in order to haze people.

   b in order to belong to something.

   c because of the mystery of the idea.

4 Which group is not mentioned as fighting hazing?

   a policing authorities

   b university personnel

   c the military

Segment Three

5 What is lacking from studies about meditation?

   a available participants

   b behavioural evidence

   c physiological studies

6 What about TM is not dissimilar to other forms of meditation?

   a the need for it to be better researched

   b its popularity with the masses

   c the amount of time it has existed

C 🔊 **12.2** Listen again and check your answers.

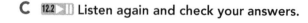

Writing: a report (2)

A Read the sample tasks and write each report's purpose, target reader and context.

Learning Reminder

Getting the most out of the prompt material
- The prompt material contains everything you need to know, so read it carefully to identify the purpose, the audience and the context of the report you will write.
- Use these elements to identify the writer's role, the correct style and language to use, and the information that you need to include.
- Instead of being given a specific subject to write about, you may need to identify two or three aspects of interest and choose one to write about. You can write a report from either a positive or negative viewpoint.

A

You work as a tour guide for a travel agency and it has asked you to write a report on tours. They would like to provide tours that offer a cultural experience for tourists. You should write a report describing the importance of including a country's culture in a tour, then give two ideas of how to achieve this. You should also evaluate the impact this would have on a tourist's overall experience in a country.

Purpose: _____

Target reader: _____

Context: _____

B

You're a receptionist at a museum which features folklore from your country's history. You need to write a report for a free brochure for museum patrons. Write a report giving basic information about folklore traditions. Then describe two aspects of the museum that patrons will find interesting. End by illustrating the kinds of folklore art still present today and why we need to preserve them.

Purpose: _____

Target reader: _____

Context: _____

C

You are participating in a research study about minority rights. The researcher has asked you to write a report about abuses of these rights. Write a report that describes the problems that minorities face and two of the ways in which their rights are infringed upon. Conclude by discussing the importance of protecting their rights and the contribution they make to a country's cultural diversity.

Purpose: _____

Target reader: _____

Context: _____

B Look back at the sample tasks in exercise A and answer the questions. More than one answer may be possible.

Which report …
1 will require the most formal language? ☐
2 might take on a negative tone? ☐
3 will be read by the most people? ☐
4 asks for solutions to an issue? ☐
5 involves a touristic context? ☐
6 will conclude with the current relevance of the subject matter? ☐

C Look back at exercise A again and match these aspects to the task they would accompany. Some aspects do not match any of the tasks.

1	Folkloric festival ☐	5	Contents of exhibitions ☐	9	Gastronomy ☐
2	Museum organisation ☐	6	All-inclusive hotels ☐	10	Exclusion from office ☐
3	Racial discrimination ☐	7	Degree in cultural studies ☐	11	Freedom of religion ☐
4	Interactive displays ☐	8	Language barriers ☐	12	Archaeology ☐

D Read and complete the *Exam Task* below. Don't forget to use the *Useful Expressions* on page 181 of your Student's Book.

Exam Task

You work for a tourism company which wants to provide some background about important people in your country's history. Write a report about a historical figure from your country for the company's website describing the details of this person's life. Then describe two aspects of this person that are most memorable. You should also explain why it is important for countries to remember significant people from their history.

Write your **report** in 280–320 words.

⤺ Writing Reference p. 208 in Student's Book

Vocabulary

A Choose the correct answers.

1 The unpopular prime minister was _____ in the press when she tripped while walking in a muddy field.

  a slandered   **b** lampooned

  c hounded   **d** stalked

2 The magazine has _____ centres in a number of European countries as well as the US and Canada.

  a instalment   **b** circulation

  c distribution   **d** correspondent

3 My husband is Scottish, but I'm mostly of German _____.

  a progeny   **b** offspring

  c descent   **d** ancestor

4 Do you think it's _____ to have the story written in less than a week?

  a acclaimed   **b** illustrious

  c credible   **d** feasible

5 We have a _____ tradition in my house of opening one present the night before Christmas.

  a level-headed   **b** deep-seated

  c time-honoured   **d** sharp-tongued

6 The singer laments how _____ was not all it was cracked up to be.

  a stardom   **b** limelight

  c comeback   **d** publicity

7 For this data, you'll need to search the _____ of years 1960 to 1962.

  a values   **b** legacies

  c annals   **d** dowries

8 Is there any particular dress _____ you would like me to adhere to?

  a mode   **b** norm

  c code   **d** law

9 After being signed by her first record _____ Kelly threw a lavish party at her own expense.

  a sticker   **b** label

  c ticket   **d** marker

10 He used a stiff brush to remove the dust from the ancient _____.

  a artefact   **b** residue

  c archive   **d** memento

11 The zero-carbon building projects in Sweden are a good _____ which other countries should follow.

  a replica   **b** model

  c copy   **d** genre

12 Dustin hasn't talked to any of his old friends since becoming famous; he's really _____ of himself now.

  a full   **b** deep

  c rich   **d** most

13 Her _____ to her mother was astonishing; they truly looked like sisters.

  a equivalence   **b** parallel

  c likeness   **d** comparison

14 Since I'm the brother of one of these contestants, I'm afraid I can't be _____ in the judging.

  a imperative   **b** impressive

  c impatient   **d** impartial

15 Rather than squabble amongst themselves, the neighbours _____ forces to fight the council.

  a banded   **b** closed

  c joined   **d** fused

16 The tragic events in the village happened so long ago, they were now lost in the _____ of time.

  a shades   **b** clouds

  c shadows   **d** mists

17 After the killing of an unarmed teen, _____ broke out in the community and the police had to be informed.

  a wars   **b** disputes

  c riots   **d** battles

18 There's no end to the kinds of antics stars will get up to in _____ publicity.

  a finding   **b** seeking

  c getting   **d** taking

19 The artist was so prolific in his youth that by the time he reached his forties, he was a living _____.

  a icon   **b** fable

  c myth   **d** legend

20 I never read those rubbish newspapers – they're full of celebrity _____ and you can't believe a word of it.

  a libel   **b** press

  c gossip   **d** chat

Grammar

B Choose the correct answers.

1 We're looking forward ____ your article in the local newspaper.
   a to read   b reading
   c to reading   d in reading

2 I think they failed ____ the significance of the news about the boom in property prices.
   a understanding   b to understand
   c understand   d to understanding

3 I'm not sure Mary can do anything with your CV; you might ____ it to her supervisor.
   a be sending   b to send
   c sending   d want to send

4 The different tribes didn't get on well and ____ they agreed on was their dislike for central government.
   a it   b what
   c all   d that

5 The ____ they don't go out on New Year's Eve is they prefer to avoid the massive crowds.
   a why   b people
   c reason   d holidays

6 I can't imagine ____ on a story that takes place in a war zone.
   a to report   b report
   c reporting   d the report

7 Cleopatra wasn't Egyptian; ____ ancient Macedonia that she originated.
   a it was where   b what was then
   c it was from   d she was from

8 Now that you don't live across the street any more, I ____ visiting you.
   a would like   b promise
   c miss   d forget

9 I don't think you should talk about work matters at a dinner party; ____ to do is relax.
   a all they want
   b what people want
   c what's
   d the only thing

10 You can flash your press pass at the door, but I'm afraid that's not enough ____ you inside.
   a to getting   b getting
   c get   d to get

11 Normandy has a well-known war memorial, for it was ____ that the troops landed in World War II.
   a that   b there
   c then   d where

12 I approached the reporter ____ that he vacate the premises.
   a requesting   b to request
   c request   d in requesting

13 Jeffrey stays out all hours of the night, and there's no ____ where he went or when he'll return.
   a accounting   b knowing
   c hoping   d pleasing

14 Joe hates using laptops, so what he ____ is he writes his novels with old-fashioned pen and paper.
   a uses   b has
   c did   d does

15 After printing lies about the celebrity, the court ____ retract the story.
   a made the paper   b made the paper to
   c was made to   d was made the paper to

16 You didn't meet me at that party; ____ my twin brother Greg at Beth's on Saturday night.
   a what was   b was it
   c all that was   d that was

17 She had no desire to interview a ruthless dictator, but she ____ do it by her publisher.
   a made   b made to
   c was made to   d was made

18 I'm sorry, but reporters from this paper are not allowed ____ the press conference.
   a attend   b to attend
   c attending   d to attending

19 If you want to be a successful journalist, you had ____ be prepared to work long hours for little pay.
   a prefer to   b like to
   c rather   d better

20 The American buffalo was hunted by both settlers and native Americans in the 1800s, and it was ____ that they were nearly driven to extinction.
   a then   b them
   c they   d there

Use of English

C Read the text below and decide which answer (a, b, c or d) best fits each gap.

Gastronomy of Greece

Greece's culinary (1) _____ can be traced back to its ancient roots and (2) _____ makes it so well-known across the globe is its numerous health benefits. There is a(n) (3) _____ tradition of incorporating fresh vegetables, whole grains and fish into a variety of meals, and the medical profession has been quite (4) _____ in its promotion of this diet.

Additionally, it has gained much (5) _____ from being featured in cooking shows internationally, and (6) _____ chefs such as Gordon Ramsay and Jamie Oliver have professed their love of Greek cuisine. The cooking traditions of the past are still (7) _____, such as the heavy use of olive oil, wheat and wine in food. One could say these ingredients are the remaining (8) _____ of an ancient method of preparing meals, which is still very relevant today.

1	a	ancestry	b	legacy	c	heritage	d chronicle
2	a	it	b	all	c	that	d what
3	a	strongly-held	b	long-standing	c	old-time	d long-gone
4	a	verbal	b	oral	c	vocal	d choral
5	a	circulation	b	press	c	distribution	d publicity
6	a	notorious	b	immortal	c	fabled	d acclaimed
7	a	observed	b	adhered	c	obeyed	d watched
8	a	heirlooms	b	relics	c	vestiges	d artefacts

D Complete the text with the correct form of the words in bold.

The good side of television

The basic (1) _____ that television is a bad influence on society might need a rethink. Studies show that audiences today are, in general, intolerant of any behaviour on television that might seem (2) _____ and thus unfair to a certain group of people. If a television show were to ascribe (3) _____ or attitudes to a character which portrayed them in a negative light based on their skin colour, origin or socio-economic status, the (4) _____ of this would create a storm on social media. This, in fact, is a positive development, as it shows that television, while being funnelled into our living rooms rather (5) _____, has done a lot to instil strong values in its viewers. Furthermore, any actors who make racist comments gain (6) _____ almost instantly. In thinking back to the shows that have been produced over the years, there are many examples of producers making (7) _____ a cornerstone of programming. Naturally, there are still features of television programming that warrant parental (8) _____ due to the impact they could have on young viewers. Overall though, it is fair to say that some aspects of television can be a powerful and positive forces in our lives.

ASSUME

STEREOTYPE

MANNER

SENSITIVE

INVADE

NOTORIOUS

DIVERSE

DISCREET

E Complete the text with one word in each gap.

The dangers of whitewashing history

Occasionally the Department of Education requests that some course materials be rewritten or replaced because some facts are
(1) _____ odds with the image the educational authorities, and to a greater degree, the current government wishes **(2)** _____ portray. It's unfathomable that such people could think there's
(3) _____ harm in rewriting history. Nonetheless, **(4)** _____ this whitewashing does is give young learners a rosy picture of their history if they read about 'workers' rather than 'slaves', or 'conflicts' rather than 'genocide'. More importantly, the events in the lead-up to these horrors would seem harmless or even justified, and it is **(5)** _____ which allows such horrors to recur. But unscrupulous officials bent on denying the truth and reinventing the past **(6)** _____ rather risk sowing the seeds of future cruelty in order to fool citizens into believing that they live in a perfect world. Besides, citizens have a way of finding out the truth anyway and they're not going to have such warm feelings once they realise that their own government misinformed **(7)** _____. In any case, officials should stop **(8)** _____ their backs on their cultural history, no matter what it comprises.

F Complete the second sentence so that it has a similar meaning to the first sentence, using the word given. Do not change the word given. You must use between three and eight words, including the word given.

1 You can't ever know what Michael is going to say next.

   no

   There's _____ will say next.

2 They're planning to hire a DJ for the event.

   involves

   The event planning _____ DJ.

3 Fjords are found in Norway, a lovely country.

   this

   Norway is lovely and it _____ fjords are found.

4 I only take one bag when I travel, whereas John takes three.

   all

   John travels with three bags, whereas when _____ one.

5 I enjoyed running into Pete the other day.

   delighted

   The other day, I _____ Pete.

6 He had no memory of his participation in the play.

   remember

   He _____ in the play.